Contents

Rounding Numbers

1 **Round…**

   a) 7.321 to…   **i)** 1 decimal place ....   **ii)** 2 decimal places ....

   b) 16.781 to…   **i)** 1 decimal place ....   **ii)** 2 decimal places ....

   c) 0.01765 to… **i)** 2 decimal places ....   **ii)** 3 decimal places ....

   d) 0.1053 to…   **i)** 1 decimal place ....   **ii)** 3 decimal places ....

   e) 7.0707 to…   **i)** 1 decimal place ....   **ii)** 2 decimal places ....

2 **Dave's weight is measured in kg to 2 decimal places. This value rounds to 68.4kg to 1 decimal place. What is the lowest and the highest possible measurements for his actual weight?**

   Lowest possible weight: ....   Highest possible weight: ....

3 **Helen's height is measured in metres to 3 decimal places. This value rounds to 1.65m to 2 decimal places. What is the lowest and the highest possible measurements for her actual height?**

   Lowest possible height: ....   Highest possible height: ....

4 **Round…**

   a) 432 to…   **i)** 1 significant figure ....   **ii)** 2 significant figures ....

   b) 9154 to…   **i)** 1 significant figure ....   **ii)** 2 significant figures ....

   c) 10 047 to…   **i)** 2 significant figures ....   **ii)** 4 significant figures ....

   d) 0.0238 to…   **i)** 1 significant figure ....   **ii)** 2 significant figures ....

   e) 0.000 1736 to… **i)** 2 significant figures ....   **ii)** 3 significant figures ....

   f) 0.010 366 to… **i)** 2 significant figures ....   **ii)** 3 significant figures ....

5 **The attendance at a pop concert was 5700 to 2 significant figures. What is the difference between the lowest possible actual attendance and the highest possible actual attendance?**

   ....

   ....

---

6 Round 135.6742 to **a)** 1 decimal place **b)** 2 decimal places **c)** 1 significant figure
   d) 2 significant figures **e)** 3 significant figures

7 Round 0.060 38 to **a)** 1 decimal place **b)** 2 decimal places **c)** 3 decimal places
   d) 1 significant figure **e)** 2 significant figures **f)** 3 significant figures

8 Fran's weight is measured in kg to 2 decimal places. This value is rounded to 47.6kg to 1 decimal place. What is the difference between her highest possible weight and her lowest possible weight?

9 **a)** Use your calculator to work out the value of $(1.46)^2 \times 6.71$. Write down all the digits on your display.
   b) Round your answer to a suitable degree of accuracy.

Peter Sherran and Peter Derych

REVISION PLUS

Edexcel
GCSE Mathematics
for A*

Workbook

Contents

Decimals

1 Complete the following table (the first row has been done for you).

	Place Value of Digits							Decimal Number
	100 Hundreds	**10** Tens	**1** Units	DECIMAL POINT •	$\frac{1}{10}$ Tenths	$\frac{1}{100}$ Hundredths	$\frac{1}{1000}$ Thousandths	
			3		4	2		3.42
a)	1	0	2		5			
b)		1	3		4	7	1	
c)								8.407
d)		9	0		0	3	1	
e)								423.008

2 Use a calculator to write the following fractions as either recurring or terminating decimals. If the decimal is recurring, place a dot (•) over the digit or digits that repeat continuously.

a) $\frac{2}{3}$ ....   b) $\frac{2}{5}$ ....   c) $\frac{1}{11}$ ....   d) $\frac{7}{9}$ ....

3 Arrange the following decimals in ascending order of value:

6.3   0.36   3.6   0.306   0.63

....

4 Convert the following recurring decimals into fractions:

a) $0.777\dot{7}...$ b) $0.6\dot{3}\ddot{6}...$

....

c) $0.8\dot{3}...$ d) $2.\dot{3}\ddot{6}...$

....

5 Write the following fractions as decimals. For each recurring decimal, place a dot (·) over the digit or digits that repeat continuously.
a) $\frac{3}{8}$ b) $\frac{2}{9}$ c) $\frac{1}{30}$ d) $\frac{22}{25}$ e) $\frac{4}{15}$

6 Arrange the following decimals in descending order:
a) 14.32   1.432   143.2   13.42   14.23   1.342   b) $3\frac{4}{5}$ 3.45   3.045 $3\frac{2}{5}$ 3.405 $3\frac{1}{20}$

7 Convert the following recurring decimals into fractions: a) $0.111\dot{1}...$ b) $0.45\dot{4}\ddot{5}...$ c) $1.\dot{4}...$

Decimals

1 Solve the following without using a calculator. Where possible show all your working.

   a) 4.7 × 10   **b)** 13.246 × 10   **c)** 0.00146 × 100   **d)** 136.3 × 1000

   ....

   e) 7.56 × 13   **f)** 4.72 × 2.3

2 If 27 × 36 = 972, write down, without doing any further calculations, the value of…

   a) 2.7 × 36 ....   **b)** 27 × 0.36 ....   **c)** 0.27 × 3.6 ....

   d) 972 ÷ 3.6 ....   **e)** 97.2 ÷ 27 ....   **f)** 9.72 ÷ 0.36 ....

3 Work out the following without using a calculator. Where possible show all your working.

   a) 16.3 ÷ 10   **b)** 0.347 ÷ 10   **c)** 14 632.4 ÷ 100   **d)** 1.2467 ÷ 1000

   ....

   e) 37.6 ÷ 8   **f)** 41.04 ÷ 1.2

4 If 72.8 ÷ 56 = 1.3, write down, without doing any further calculations, the value of…

   a) 72.8 ÷ 5.6 ....   **b)** 7.28 ÷ 56 ....   **c)** 72.8 ÷ 0.56 ....

   d) 56 × 13 ....   **e)** 5.6 × 1.3 ....   **f)** 130 × 5.6

5 A school holds a raffle. The three prizes cost £24.65, £17.99 and £9.89. 130 tickets were sold at £1.25 each. How much profit did the school make from the raffle?

6 Jim is going to hire a cement mixer. The cost is £24.50 for the first day and £3.75 for each extra day. Jim wants to hire it for seven days. How much will it cost him in total?

7 A sports club holds a raffle. The three prizes cost £9.49, £14.99 and £19.99. Tickets cost 75p each. What is the minimum number of tickets that need to be sold for the sports club to make a profit?

8 Jean is going to hire a wallpaper stripper. The cost is £8.50 for the first day and £1.25 for each extra day. When she returns the wallpaper stripper the total hire charge is £24.75. For how many days did she hire the wallpaper stripper?

Number Properties

1 **Here are eight numbers:**

3   4   6   7   11   15   20   21

a) Which three numbers are even numbers? ....

b) Which two numbers are factors of 40? ....

c) Which two numbers are factors of 45? ....

d) Which four numbers are factors of 42? ....

e) Which two numbers are multiples of 7? ....

f) Which three numbers are multiples of 2? ....

g) Which three numbers are prime numbers? ....

h) Which number has an odd number of factors? ....

2 **Here are ten numbers:**

5   8   11   19   22   24   31   36   47   81

a) Which six numbers are odd numbers? ....

b) Which three numbers are factors of 72? ....

c) Which three numbers are factors of 110? ....

d) Which three numbers are multiples of 3? ....

e) Which three numbers are multiples of 4? ....

f) Which five numbers are prime numbers? ....

g) Which two numbers have an odd number of factors? ....

3 **What is the reciprocal of the following numbers?**

a) 8 ....
b) 0.5 ....
c) $\frac{3}{4}$ ....
d) $2\frac{1}{3}$ ....

4 **The reciprocal of a number is 0.1. Work out the number.** ....

5 **Express the following numbers in prime factor form:**

a) 36

b) 64

c) 930

....

....

....

Number Properties

6 **a)** What is the highest common factor of 20 and 36?

b) What is the lowest common multiple of 20 and 36?

7 **a)** What is the highest common factor of 64 and 100?

b) What is the lowest common multiple of 64 and 100?

8 What is **a)** the highest common factor and **b)** the lowest common multiple of 6, 15 and 24?

9 **a)** The highest common factor of two numbers is 4. The lowest common multiple of the same two numbers is 60. There are two possible solutions. Give one.

b) The highest common factor of three numbers is 15. The lowest common multiple of the same three numbers is 90. What are the three numbers?

---

10 **Here are ten numbers:**
9, 14, 25, 29, 41, 50, 61, 70, 84, 100
a) Which three numbers are: **i)** factors of 200 **ii)** multiples of 25 **iii)** multiples of 7 **iv)** prime numbers?
b) Which of the above numbers has the reciprocal 0.02?

11 **What is the reciprocal of a)** 100 **b)** $\frac{1}{100}$ **c)** 0.01 **d)** $\frac{99}{100}$?

12 **Express the following numbers in prime factor form: a)** 30 **b)** 100 **c)** 2048

13 **What is the highest common factor and lowest common multiple of...**
a) 15 and 18 **b)** 40 and 58 **c)** 15, 18 and 24?

Powers

1 **Work out the value of...**

a) 2^3 ....

b) 3^0 ....

c) 4^3 ....

d) 10^3 ....

e) 3^4 ....

f) 1^5 ....

g) $(4.5)^0$ ....

h) $(2.5)^2$ ....

2 **Here are ten numbers:**

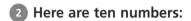

10   18   25   27   45   64   80   125   133   196

a) Which three numbers are square numbers?

....

b) Which three numbers are cube numbers?

....

c) Which one of these numbers is a square number and a cube number?

....

d) Which of the above numbers is equal to $10^2 - 6^2$?

....

e) Which of the above numbers is equal to $4^3 + 2^4$?

....

3 **Work out the value of...**

a) $(-3)^2$ ....

b) $(-3)^3$ ....

c) $(-5)^2$ ....

d) $(-5)^3$ ....

e) $(-1)^2$ ....

f) $(-1)^3$ ....

g) $(-3)^4$ ....

h) $(-10)^6$ ....

Powers

4 Work out the value of...

a) $2^3 \times 2^2$ ....

b) $3^{-2} \times 3^1$ ....

c) $4^3 \times 4^2 \times 4^1$ ....

d) $2^3 \div 2^2$ ....

e) $10^4 \div 10^2$ ....

f) $6^4 \div 6^0$ ....

g) 6^{-2} ....

h) $(4^3)^2$ ....

i) $(10^2)^3$ ....

j) $(2^2 \times 2^3)^2$ ....

k) $\dfrac{10^2 - 6^2}{4^3}$ ....

l) $\dfrac{4^3 + 2^6}{8^2}$ ....

5 Say whether the following are true or false. If false, what should the symbol be?

a) $2^3 < 3^2$ ....

b) $5^{-2} > 0.1$ ....

c) $\sqrt[3]{64} = 16^{\frac{1}{2}}$ ....

d) $10^{-2} < \dfrac{1}{100}$ ....

6 What power makes these true?

a) $2^n = 128$ ....

b) $2^n = \dfrac{1}{8}$ ....

c) $1000^n = 10$ ....

7 Work out the value of...

a) $16^{\frac{3}{4}}$ ....

b) $100\,000^{\frac{4}{5}}$ ....

c) $1024^{\frac{2}{5}}$ ....

d) $1^{\frac{9}{10}}$ ....

8 Work out the value of...

a) 4^4　b) 4^1　c) $4^4 \times 4^1$　d) $4^3 \times 5^2$　e) $8^0 + 3^3$　f) $6^2 - 3^2$　g) $\dfrac{8^2}{2^5}$　h) $\dfrac{3^3 - 7^1}{2^2}$　i) $\dfrac{10^2 + 3^3 + 5^0}{8^2}$

9 a) What is $3^3 \times 9^2$ as a single power of 3?　b) What is $5^2 - 3^2$ as a single power of 2?

c) What is $8^2 \times 2^4$ as a single power of 4?

Roots

1 **Work out the value of...**

a) $\sqrt{25}$ ....

b) $36^{\frac{1}{2}}$ ....

c) $36^{-\frac{1}{2}}$ ....

d) $196^{\frac{1}{2}}$ ....

e) $64^{\frac{1}{3}}$ ....

f) $\sqrt[3]{1}$ ....

g) $8^{-\frac{1}{3}}$ ....

h) $\sqrt[3]{-1000}$ ....

i) $27^{-\frac{2}{3}}$ ....

2 **Here are ten numbers:**

2   4   5   8   10   20   27   36   64   80

a) Which three numbers have an integer square root? ....

b) Which three numbers have an integer cube root? ....

c) Which one of these numbers has an integer square root and an integer cube root? ....

d) Which of these numbers is equal to $\sqrt{144} - 8^{\frac{1}{3}}$? ....

e) Which of these numbers is equal to $81^{\frac{1}{2}} \times \sqrt{16}$? ....

3 **Work out the value of...**

a) $(\sqrt{4})^2$ ....

b) $(5^{-4})^{\frac{1}{2}}$ ....

c) $\sqrt{4^2 \times 25}$ ....

d) $100^{\frac{1}{2}} \times \sqrt[3]{27}$ ....

e) $64^{\frac{1}{2}} \times \sqrt[3]{64}$ ....

f) $16^{\frac{3}{2}}$ ....

4 a) What is $\sqrt{4} \times 8$ as a single power of 4? ....

b) What is $\sqrt[3]{27} \times 3$ as a single power of 3? ....

c) What is $\sqrt[3]{64} \times 16^{\frac{1}{2}}$ as a single power of 2? ....

d) What is $\sqrt{9} \times 1^3 \times \sqrt{144}$ as a single power of 6? ....

5 **Find the value of x to make these true.**

a) $144^{\frac{1}{x}} = 12$ ....

b) $\sqrt[x]{64} = 4$ ....

6 **Simplify the following surds:**

a) $\sqrt{54}$ ....

b) $\sqrt{90}$ ....

c) $\dfrac{\sqrt{15}}{\sqrt{3}}$ ....

d) $(5 - \sqrt{7})^2$ ....

7 a) Rationalise the denominator of $\dfrac{4}{\sqrt{7}}$

b) Rationalise the denominator of $\dfrac{5}{\sqrt{11}}$

8 **Work out the value of...**

a) $169^{\frac{1}{2}}$ b) $\sqrt[3]{125}$ c) $\sqrt{81}$ d) $125^{\frac{1}{3}}$ e) $225^{\frac{1}{2}}$

9 **Find the value of...**

a) $(\sqrt{9})^3$ b) $(\sqrt[3]{8})^2$ c) $\sqrt[3]{6^2 + 28}$ d) $8^{-\frac{2}{3}}$ e) $64^{\frac{2}{3}}$

10 **Simplify the following surds:**

a) $\sqrt{200}$ b) $\sqrt{80}$ c) $\sqrt{63}$ d) $(5 + \sqrt{7})(5 - \sqrt{7})$ e) $(2 + \sqrt{3})(2 - \sqrt{3})^2$

Order of Operations

1 Calculate the following:

a) $7 + 5 \times 2$

....

....

b) $14 \times (5 - 3) \div 4$

....

....

c) $6^2 + 4 \times 2$

....

....

d) $\dfrac{15}{3} + 6$

....

....

e) $18 \times 2 - 5^2$

....

....

f) $\dfrac{30}{6} - \dfrac{40}{10}$

....

....

g) $2^3 + 4^3 \times 3$

....

....

h) $6 \times 7 - (10 \times 3 + 8)$

....

....

i) $15 - 3 \times 6 \times 2 + 5$

....

....

2 **a)** Put brackets in the following expression so that its value is 43:

$$13 - 3 \times 4 + 3$$

b) Put brackets in the following expression so that its value is -8:

$$13 - 3 \times 4 + 3$$

c) Put brackets in the following expression so that its value is 70:

$$13 - 3 \times 4 + 3$$

d) Put brackets in the following expression so that its value is 4:

$$13 - 3 \times 4 + 3$$

e) Put brackets in the following expression so that its value is 20.5:

$$3 \times 1.4 + 4 \times 2.5$$

f) Put brackets in the following expression so that its value is 12.12:

$$7 + 3.2 \times 6 - 4.4$$

3 Calculate the following:
a) $4 + 3 \times 13$ **b)** $4 \times 3 - 13$ **c)** $4 - 3 \times 13$ **d)** $4^2 \div 2 + 3$ **e)** $9 + 15 \div 5$ **f)** $4 + 7 \times 3 - 15$
g) $14 \div 4 - 5$ **h)** $3 \times (7 - 5) \times 3^2$ **i)** $5 + 6 \times (3 - 8)$

4 Put brackets in the following expression so that its value is... **a)** -1   **b)** 35   **c)** -51

$$3^2 - 4 \times 5 + 10$$

5 Put brackets in the following expression so that its value is... **a)** 54   **b)** -2   **c)** 6

$$4^2 - 3 \times 4 + 2$$

Standard Index Form

1 Write the following numbers (currently in standard index form) as ordinary numbers:

a) 2.3×10^{2} ....

b) 2.3×10^{3} ....

c) 4.21×10^{4} ....

d) 6.32×10^{1} ....

e) 7.467×10^{3} ....

f) 3×10^{2} ....

g) 2.3×10^{3} ....

h) 4.21×10^{-4} ....

i) 6.324×10^{-2} ....

2 Write the following numbers in standard index form:

a) 600 ....

b) 473 ....

c) 42000 ....

d) 413 256 ....

e) 496.3 ....

f) 0.032 ....

g) 0.47 ....

h) 0.000 631 ....

i) 0.1 ....

3 The number of seconds in one year is approximately 3.1×10^{7}. Use this number to answer the following questions.

a) How many seconds are there in 5 years? Give your answer in standard index form.

....

b) On her next birthday Chloe has calculated that she will be 4.34×10^{8} seconds old!
How old will Chloe be in years?

....

c) How many seconds are there from Chloe's next birthday until her 21st birthday?
Give your answer in standard index form.

....

....

4 Calculate the following. Give your answers in standard index form.

a) $9.23 \times 10^{2} + 4.71 \times 10^{3}$ ....

b) $7.15 \times 10^{5} - 9.68 \times 10^{4}$ ....

c) $2.34 \times 10^{4} \times 3.6 \times 10^{7}$ ....

d) $5.5 \times 10^{7} \div 1.1 \times 10^{9}$ ....

5 Write these values in order, smallest first: 8.14×10^{7}, 7.49×10^{6}, 2.43×10^{8}, 9.34×10^{6}

6 In one minute light will travel a distance of approximately 1.8×10^{10} metres. (Give your answers to a), b) and d) in standard index form.)

a) How far will light travel in 1 hour? **b)** How far will light travel in 1 year? **c)** The Sun is approximately 1.44×10^{11} metres away. How long does it take light to travel from the Sun to the Earth? **d)** A light year is the distance travelled by light in 1 Earth year. Our nearest star, after the Sun, is 4.3 light years away. How far away is this star in metres?

Fractions

1 **Here are eight fractions:**

$$\frac{35}{50} \qquad \frac{16}{40} \qquad \frac{60}{90} \qquad \frac{28}{40} \qquad \frac{30}{40} \qquad \frac{40}{100} \qquad \frac{84}{120} \qquad \frac{10}{25}$$

a) Which three fractions are equivalent to $\frac{2}{5}$? ....

b) Which three fractions are equivalent to $\frac{7}{10}$? ....

2 **Express the following fractions in their simplest form:**

a) $\frac{27}{30}$ .... **b)** $\frac{42}{6}$ .... **c)** $\frac{84}{105}$ .... **d)** $\frac{108}{184}$ ....

3 **a)** Arrange the following fractions in ascending order:

$$\frac{5}{6} \qquad \frac{3}{5} \qquad \frac{11}{15} \qquad \frac{2}{3} \qquad \frac{1}{2}$$

....

b) Arrange the following fractions in descending order:

$$\frac{9}{40} \qquad \frac{3}{5} \qquad \frac{5}{8} \qquad \frac{9}{10} \qquad \frac{1}{4}$$

....

4 **Find the fraction that is halfway between the following:**

a) $\frac{4}{5}$ and $\frac{9}{10}$ .... **b)** $\frac{5}{12}$ and $\frac{9}{20}$ ....

5 **Write down two fractions that are greater than $\frac{7}{10}$ but less than $\frac{5}{6}$.**

....

6 **a)** Write the following improper fractions as mixed numbers:

i) $\frac{11}{5}$ .... **ii)** $\frac{13}{6}$ .... **iii)** $\frac{24}{5}$ .... **iv)** $\frac{32}{3}$ ....

b) Write the following mixed numbers as improper fractions:

i) $3\frac{1}{3}$ .... **ii)** $5\frac{1}{4}$ .... **iii)** $11\frac{3}{5}$ .... **iv)** $20\frac{1}{20}$ ....

7 Write down three fractions that are equivalent to each of the following: **a)** $\frac{2}{3}$ **b)** $\frac{4}{7}$ **c)** $\frac{9}{11}$

8 Express the following fractions in their simplest form and then arrange them into ascending order:

$$\frac{28}{35} \qquad \frac{38}{40} \qquad \frac{75}{100} \qquad \frac{42}{84} \qquad \frac{99}{110}$$

9 Write down three fractions that are greater than $\frac{4}{5}$ but less than $\frac{9}{10}$.

Calculations with Fractions

1. Work out the following without using a calculator. Show all your working and give your answers in their simplest form.

a) $\frac{3}{4} + \frac{2}{3}$ ....

b) $\frac{2}{9} + \frac{7}{8}$ ....

c) $4\frac{1}{2} + 2\frac{9}{10}$ ....

d) $7\frac{5}{8} + 4\frac{1}{3}$ ....

e) $\frac{9}{10} - \frac{1}{2}$ ....

f) $\frac{13}{15} - \frac{2}{3}$ ....

g) $4\frac{4}{5} - 1\frac{3}{8}$ ....

h) $9\frac{1}{6} - 4\frac{3}{5}$ ....

2. At a football match $\frac{5}{12}$ of the crowd is over 40 years old, $\frac{1}{4}$ of the crowd is between 20 years old and 40 years old, and the remainder of the crowd is less than 20 years old.

What fraction of the crowd is less than 20 years old? Give your answer in its simplest form.

....

....

....

3. Work out the following without using a calculator. Show all your working and give your answers in their simplest form.

a) $\frac{1}{4} \times \frac{2}{5}$ ....

b) $\frac{9}{10} \times \frac{2}{7}$ ....

c) $\frac{3}{4} \div \frac{9}{10}$ ....

d) $\frac{7}{8} \div \frac{7}{12}$ ....

e) $3\frac{1}{2} \times 1\frac{3}{5}$ ....

f) $3\frac{1}{4} \times 1\frac{5}{7}$ ....

g) $4\frac{1}{2} \div 2\frac{2}{3}$ ....

h) $1\frac{1}{2} \div 2\frac{1}{4}$ ....

i) $\frac{8}{9} \times 4$ ....

j) $\frac{7}{10} \div 3$ ....

---

4. Work out the following without using a calculator. Show all your working.

a) $\frac{7}{10} + \frac{5}{8}$ b) $2\frac{1}{3} + 4\frac{3}{8}$ c) $\frac{9}{10} - \frac{2}{3}$ d) $4\frac{1}{2} - 3\frac{7}{10}$ e) $\frac{2}{5} \times \frac{7}{10}$ f) $\frac{13}{15} \div \frac{4}{5}$

g) $3\frac{1}{4} \times 1\frac{2}{3}$ h) $4\frac{1}{5} \div 3\frac{1}{2}$ i) $4\frac{1}{2} \times 5$ j) $2\frac{1}{3} \div 6$

Calculation with Fractions

1 James wants to buy an MP3 player that costs £240.

He pays $\frac{1}{8}$ of the cost as a deposit. How much deposit did James pay?

....

....

2 Mary buys a new car that costs £13 000.

She pays $\frac{2}{5}$ of the cost as a deposit. She pays the remainder monthly over a period of four years.

a) How much deposit does Mary pay?

....

....

b) What is her monthly repayment?

....

....

c) At the end of the four years Mary decides to sell her car. It is now worth £7150. Express its value now, after four years, as a fraction of its value when new. Give your answer in its simplest form.

....

....

3 A shop holds a sale where all items are reduced by $\frac{1}{6}$.

a) Calculate the sale price of an item that cost £93.60 before the sale.

....

....

b) The sale price of another item is £121.50. Calculate its price before it was reduced.

....

....

---

4 A football match lasts $1\frac{1}{2}$ hours. During the match, player number 9 sits on the bench for a total of 15 minutes. He is on the pitch for the rest of the time. Express the total length of time that player number 9 is on the pitch as a fraction of the time that the match lasts. Give your answer in its simplest form.

5 In a sale, a washing machine has its original price reduced by $\frac{1}{2}$. The following week the sale price is further reduced by $\frac{1}{4}$.

a) If the washing machine originally cost £600, calculate its sale price after **i)** the first reduction, **ii)** the second reduction.

b) If a washing machine in the same sale costs £150 after both reductions what was its original price?

6 Express 40 seconds as a fraction of 1 hour.

Percentages

1 **Arrange in order of size (smallest first):**

a) 0.38, $\frac{6}{16}$, 4% ....

b) $\frac{11}{15}$, 0.75, $\frac{2}{3}$, 70% ....

2 **Calculate the following amounts:**

a) 20% of 60p ....

b) 30% of 6.5km ....

3 **Express...**

a) £18 as a percentage of £90 ....

b) 42cm as a percentage of 8.4m ....

4 **Alan has kept a record of his height and weight from when he was aged 10 and aged 16.**

Aged 10	1.2m tall	40kg weight
Aged 16	1.74m tall	64kg weight

a) i) Calculate the increase in his height from the age of 10 to aged 16. ....

ii) Express this increase as a percentage of his height at the age of 10. ....

b) i) Calculate the increase in his weight from the age of 10 to aged 16. ....

ii) Express this increase as a percentage of his weight at the age of 10. ....

5 **A train ticket costs £17.60 when bought on the day of travel. If the same ticket is bought in advance it costs £15.40. Express the saving you make when you buy the ticket in advance as a percentage of the full ticket price when bought on the day of travel.**

....

....

6 **Calculate the following amounts:**
a) 45% of £2.60 **b)** 80% of 6.4kg **c)** 5% of £10.40.

7 **a)** Express 46cm as a percentage of 69cm **b)** Express 200m as a percentage of 200km **c)** Express 550g as a percentage of 2kg.

8 **A tin of tomato soup weighs 420g. Special tins weigh 546g. Calculate the increase in the weight of a special tin as a percentage of the weight of a normal tin.**

9 **A brand new car bought in the UK costs £18 000. The same car bought abroad costs £14 850. Calculate the decrease in the price when the car is bought abroad as a percentage of its price in the UK.**

Percentage Change

1 A brand new car costs £15 000. It is estimated that it will decrease in value by 23% in the first year. What is the estimated value of the car at the end of the first year?

....

....

2 The average attendance at a football club over a season was 32 500. In the next season there was a 6% increase in the average attendance. What was the average attendance for that season?

....

....

3 Mr and Mrs Smith bought a house for £120 000. Every subsequent year the value of the property increases by 10%.

a) Calculate the value of the house two years after they bought it.

....

....

b) The value of the house after two years can be found by multiplying the original cost by a single number. What is this number as a decimal?

....

4 Jim buys a new motorbike for £10 000.

a) If the value of the motorbike decreases by 20% each year, calculate the value of the motorbike after three years.

....

....

b) The value of Jim's bike after three years can be found by multiplying the original cost by a single number. What is this number as a decimal?

....

5 An electrical shop has a sale. All items are reduced by 20%. The following week the shop takes 10% off its sale prices. Pat wants to buy a fridge that was priced at £100 before the sale. She reckons that she will save 30% of this price and that the fridge will now cost her £70. Is she correct? Explain why.

6 Bob weighs 120kg on the 1st of January. Over the first six months of the year his weight increases by 5%. Over the next six months his weight decreases by 10%.
a) What is his weight at the end of the year?
b) Bob's weight at the end of the year can be found by multiplying his weight on the 1st of January by a single number. What is this number as a decimal?

1 Phil has been told by his mum that he needs to spend 1 hour a day doing his homework, an increase of 50%. How long did Phil originally spend doing his homework each day?

....

2 An electrical shop has a sale. All items are reduced by 15%. A tumble dryer has a sale price of £122.40. What was the price of the tumble dryer before the sale?

....

....

3 A man buys an antique clock. He later sells it for £5040, an increase of 12% on the price he paid for it. How much did the clock cost him?

....

....

4 Dave is a long distance lorry driver. On Tuesday he drives 253km. This is a 15% increase on the distance he drove the previous day. How far did he drive on Monday?

....

....

5 Jean has her house valued. It is worth £84 000. This is a 40% increase on the price she originally paid for it. How much did Jean pay for her house?

....

....

6 The price of a house was £90 000. At the end of each year the price increases by 6%. Find the price after...
a) 1 year   b) 3 years   c) 10 years

7 A new car is valued at £15000. At the end of each year its value has reduced by 15% (of its value at the start of the year). What will the car be worth after the following?
a) 2 years   b) 3 years   c) 5 years

8 A clothes shop has a sale. All prices are reduced by 30%. The sale price of a dress is £86.80. What was the original price of the dress?

9 Mrs Smith buys some shares. In twelve months their value has increased by 15% to £3680. How much did she pay for the shares?

10 Mr Jones collects stamps. After two years he has increased the number of stamps in his collection by 120% to 660. How many stamps did he have in his collection two years ago?

11 Mrs Galloway wants to invest £20 000 for 3 years. She can either invest it at 6% simple interest or 5.5% compound interest. Which option will make the most money?

Ratios

1 **Jim weighs 70kg. His sister Cathy weighs 35kg.**

   a) Calculate the ratio of Jim's weight to Cathy's weight in its simplest form.

   ....

   b) Express your answer to part **a)** in the form $1 : n$. ....

2 **Freya is 90cm tall. Her brother Tom is 1.35m tall.**

   a) Calculate the ratio of Freya's height to Tom's height in its simplest form.

   ....

   b) Express your answer to part **a)** in the form $1 : n$. ....

3 $\frac{3}{7}$ **of the teachers at a school are male.**

   a) What is the ratio of male teachers to female teachers? ....

   b) Express your answer to part **a)** in the form $1 : n$. ....

4 **A large tin of baked beans costs 36p and weighs 450g. A small tin of baked beans costs 22p and weighs 250g.**

   a) Calculate the ratio of the weight of the two tins in its simplest form. ....

   b) Calculate the ratio of the cost of the two tins in its simplest form. ....

   c) Which tin represents the best value for money? Explain your answer.

   ....

   ....

5 **a)** Divide 80p in the ratio of 2 : 3   **b)** Divide 6.3m in the ratio 2 : 3 : 4

   ....

   ....

6 **£5000 is shared between three women in the ratio of their ages. Their combined age is 120 years. If Susan gets £2500, Janet gets £1500 and Polly gets the remainder, what are their ages?**

   ....

   ....

   ....

7 **A dealer values 3 caravans according to the ratio of the lengths, which are 4.5m, 5.7m and 6.3m. If the shortest caravan is priced at £3750, what price is he asking for the other two?**

   ....

   ....

Calculations with Ratios

1 In a maths class there are 30 pupils on the register and the ratio of girls to boys is 3 : 2. If 4 girls and 2 boys are absent from the class, what does the ratio of girls to boys become?

....

....

....

2 A builder makes concrete by mixing cement, gravel, sand and water in the ratio 2 : 8 : 5 : 3 by weight. How many kilograms of sand, to the nearest kg, does he need to make 10 000kg of concrete?

....

....

....

3 Opposite is a recipe for making 10 biscuits.

a) Calculate the amount of each ingredient needed to make 25 biscuits.

....

....

....

....

> **Recipe**
> 90g of flour
> 130g oatmeal
> 80g margarine

b) How many biscuits can be made using 0.715kg of oatmeal?

....

....

....

....

4 100ml of semi-skimmed milk contains 4.8g carbohydrate and 1.8g fat.
a) What is the ratio of carbohydrate to fat? **b)** Express your answer to part a) in the form 1 : *n*.

5 A large tub of margarine weighs 500g and costs £1.10. A small tub of margarine that normally weighs 250g has an extra 10% free and costs 52p. Which tub of margarine represents the best value for money? Explain your answer.

6 450 tickets were sold for a raffle at 20p each. The ratio of the cost of prizes to profit made is 5 : 13. How much profit did the raffle make?

7 The angles of a quadrilateral are in the ratio 2 : 3 : 5 : 8. What is the size of the largest angle?

8 A large packet of washing powder weighs 2.5kg and costs £5.60. How much should a 750g packet of washing powder cost if it represents the same value for money as the large packet?

9 A map has a scale of 1 : 50000.
a) On the map a road measures 3.5cm. How long is the road in km?
b) What would the measurement be on the map if a railway line stretches for 2700m in real life?

Direct and Inverse Proportion

1 y is directly proportional to x^2 and $y = 16$ when $x = 8$.

   a) What is the value of y when $x = 12$?

   ....

   ....

   ....

   ....

   b) What is the value of x when $y = 100$?

   ....

   ....

   ....

   ....

2 y is inversely proportional to x^2 and $y = 4$ when $x = 3$.

   a) What is the value of y when $x = 6$?

   ....

   ....

   ....

   b) What is the value of x when $y = 12$?

   Leave your answer in surd form.

   ....

   ....

   ....

3 The volume, V, of a sphere is directly proportional to the cube of its radius, r. If a sphere has a volume of 33.6cm³ when its radius is 2cm, calculate the radius of a sphere of volume 14.175cm³.

....

....

....

....

4 The pressure, P, exerted by a constant force is inversely proportional to the area, A, over which the force acts. If the pressure exerted is 15N/cm² when the area is 12cm², calculate the pressure exerted when the area is 9cm².

....

....

....

....

5 a is directly proportional to bc and $a = 120$ when $b = 6$ and $c = 4$
   a) Calculate the value of a when $b = 10$ and $c = 6$
   b) Calculate the value of b when $a = 66$ and $c = 1.2$

6 m is inversely proportional to the cube of n and $m = 20$ when $n = 0.8$
   a) Calculate the value of m when $n = 1.6$
   b) Calculate the value of n when $m = 20\,000$

1 a) Some ribbon is measured as 7.4cm to the nearest mm. What are the upper and lower bounds of the length of the ribbon?

....

b) Kevin cuts a length of ribbon measuring 3.2cm to the nearest mm. Find the greatest and shortest length of ribbon remaining.

....

2 The weight of a BMW car is given as 1900kg to the nearest 100kg. Find the difference between the greatest and least possible weight of this car as a percentage of the given weight (to 2 s.f.).

....

3 Ellie measured the length and width of the cover of a book (her measurements are accurate to 1 d.p.).

a) What is the greatest possible length of the cover of the book?

....

b) Find the shortest possible length of the cover of the book.

....

c) Between what bounds must the width of the cover lie?

....

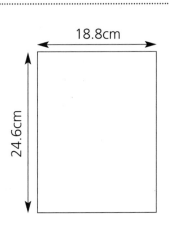

18.8cm

24.6cm

4 A floor is measured as 3.8m × 4.9m to the nearest 10cm.

a) Calculate the largest possible area of floor.

....

b) Calculate the smallest possible area of floor.

....

c) As an inequality, write down the range of possible values for the actual area of floor.

....

d) Calculate the upper and lower bounds of the perimeter of the floor.

....

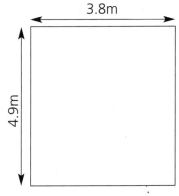

3.8m

4.9m

5 Julie measures the length and width of a sheet of A4 paper, the dimensions are given opposite. She then cuts out a circle of radius 7cm. All measurements are to the nearest cm. Find **a)** the greatest possible area of paper left **b)** the least possible area of paper left.

30cm

21cm

6 A car travels at an average speed of 37.6 miles per hour over a distance of 53.2 miles. Both measurements are correct to 1 d.p. Calculate the range of possible values for the time taken (to 2 s.f.).

Estimating and Checking

1 **a)** **i)** Without using a calculator estimate the answer to 106 × 53

....

ii) Work out the actual answer using a calculator. ....

b) **i)** Without using a calculator estimate the answer to 3.8 × 15.2

....

ii) Work out the actual answer using a calculator. ....

c) **i)** Without using a calculator estimate the answer to $\dfrac{29.4 \times 5.8}{19.6}$

....

ii) Work out the actual answer using a calculator. ....

d) **i)** Without using a calculator estimate the answer to 384 726 × 0.000 71

....

ii) Work out the actual answer using a calculator. ....

2 John and Donna collect and keep all their loose change. The table below shows how much they collected for three successive months.

MONTH	JOHN	DONNA
JUNE	£7.36	£9.10
JULY	£8.90	£16.58
AUGUST	£13.47	£4.52

a) John has calculated that he has collected £29.73 altogether.

i) Check by estimation whether he is likely to be correct.

....

ii) Check John's calculation for accuracy.

....

b) Donna has calculated that she has collected £34.20 altogether.

i) Check by estimation whether she is likely to be correct.

....

ii) Check Donna's calculation for accuracy.

....

3 Check the following calculations by estimation and then for accuracy. Make any necessary corrections.
   a) 13 + 29 + 43 = 82   **b)** 9.06 + 11.58 + 7.23 + 13.86 = 41.73
   c) (3 × 6.25) + 92 − 10 = 101.75   **d)** (4.7 × 6.3) + (0.8 × 9.5) = 40.21

1 **Simplify...**

a) $9p - 2p + 4p$

b) $3a^2 - 2a^2$

c) $10w^2 - w^2 + 2w^2$

d) $2a + 3b + 4a + 5b$

e) $7c - 8d - 9c + 10d$

f) $4ab + 8cd - 7ba + cd + ab$

g) $-4x^2 + 6x + 7 + 3x^2 - 11x + 2$

h) $14 - 8p^2 + 11p + 2p^2 - 4p + 3$

i) $3a \times 2b$

j) $12pq \times 2r$

k) $4st \times 3st^2$

l) $\dfrac{6bc^2 \times 3b^2}{2abc}$

2 **Explain why $2x + 3x = 5x$ is an example of an identity and not an equation.**

3 **Simplify...**

a) $a^2 \times a^3$

b) $4b^3 \times 3b$

c) $6p^4q \times 4qp$

d) $r^6 \div r^2$

e) $12c^4 \div 3c^3$

f) $18a^2b \div 9a$

g) $15a^3b^2 \div 3ab$

h) $(2a^2b)^3$

i) $5p(2pq^3)^2$

4 **Simplify...**

a) $\dfrac{8ab^2}{4b}$

b) $\dfrac{16a^3b^2}{ab^2}$

c) $\dfrac{(4ab)^2}{2ab^2}$

d) $\dfrac{12bc^2 \times 3ab^2}{4abc}$

5 **Simplify...**

a) $(n^6)^{\frac{1}{4}}$

b) $(a^{-5})^2$

c) $\sqrt{36n^4}$

6 **Simplify...**

a) $12x + 6x$ b) $12x - 6x$ c) $12x \times 6x$ d) $12x \div 6x$ e) $4p^2 - 11p^2$

f) $19ab - 13bc + 2ab + 16bc$ g) $13ab + 4a^2b - 2ab^2 + 3a^2b - 4ab + 10ab^2$

7 **Simplify...**

a) $a^4 \times a^3 \times a^2$ b) $2x^2 \times 3x \times 5x^5$ c) $16x^4 \div 16x^2$ d) $20a^3b^2c \div 10a^2b$ e) $(4a^2)^3$ f) $(3a^2b)^4$

8 **Use the identity $(x + 3)^2 = x^2 + 6x + 9$ to solve the equation $x^2 + 7x + 9 = (x + 3)^2 + 11$**

Substitution

1 If $p = 2$, $q = 5$ and $r = -4$, find the value of...

a) $2p + 3q$ ....

b) $2(p + q)$ ....

c) $2pq$ ....

d) p^2q ....

e) $pq - q^2$ ....

f) pqr ....

g) $p^3 + r^2$ ....

h) $\dfrac{4p}{r}$ ....

i) $p^2q^2 + \dfrac{r}{p}$ ....

j) $\dfrac{p}{q} + \dfrac{r}{q}$ ....

2 If $x = \dfrac{1}{2}$, $y = \dfrac{1}{3}$ and $z = -2$, find the value of...

a) $x + y$ ....

b) xz ....

c) xz^2 ....

d) $\dfrac{1}{x} + z$ ....

3 Find the value of...

a) $3x - 7$ when $x = -3$ ....

b) $4(x^2 - 1)$ when $x = -3$ ....

c) $4(x - 1)^2$ when $x = 5$ ....

d) $(x + 2)(x - 3)$ when $x = 6$ ....

e) $(x^2 - 5)(x + 8)$ when $x = -5$ ....

---

4 If $e = 3$, $f = 8$, $g = -4$ and $h = \dfrac{1}{4}$, find the value of...

a) ef **b)** fg **c)** gh **d)** $e + f + g$ **e)** $f + g + h$ **f)** $e^2 - f$ **g)** g^2h **h)** $\dfrac{f}{g}$ **i)** $e^3 + g$ **j)** $\dfrac{2f}{g^2}$ **k)** $\dfrac{1}{e} + h$ **l)** $e^2 + f + g^2$

5 Find the value of...
a) $5x^2 - 3$ when $x = -4$ **b)** $5(x - 3)$ when $x = -4$ **c)** $5x^2 - 3$ when $x = -2$ **d)** $(x + 3)(2x - 1)$ when $x = 2$
e) $(x^2 + 3)(x - 5)$ when $x = -1$

6 If $m = 3 \times 10^4$ and $n = 5 \times 10^3$, find the value of...
a) mn **b)** $m + n$ **c)** $\dfrac{mn}{m + n}$

Give your answers in standard form to 2 significant figures.

Brackets and Factorisation

1 Expand and simplify...

a) $4(2x + 1)$

b) $3(3r - 7)$

c) $2m(3m + 2)$

d) $2p(4 - p)$

e) $6r(r^2 - 3)$

f) $10x(4x^2 - 3x)$

g) $5(2y + 4) + 3$

h) $5x(2 - 3x) + 7x$

i) $11x(5 - 3x^2) - 9x$

j) $5(3x + 2) + 4(x - 3)$

k) $5(6x + 1) + 3(4x - 2)$

l) $5x(2x - 3) - 4(3x - 1)$

m) $(x + 2)(x + 5)$

n) $(2x + 3)(x + 4)$

o) $(3x - 2)(2x + 1)$

p) $(4x - 1)(x - 5)$

q) $(x + 3)(x - 3)$

r) $(4x - 1)^2$

2 Factorise the following expressions:

a) $5x + 10$

b) $4x - 8$

c) $6x + 10y$

d) $6x + 3x^2$

e) $10x^2 - 5x$

f) $6x^2y - 10xy$

g) $4p^2q^3r + 6pqr$

h) $x(3y + 2) + z(3y + 2)$

i) $x(4y + 3) + (4y + 3)^2$

3 Expand and simplify...
a) $6(4x - y)$ **b)** $3x(2x + 5)$ **c)** $4x^2(2y - x)$ **d)** $6x(3 - x^2)$ **e)** $4(2x + 3) + 5(x - 7)$ **f)** $6x(2x - 3) + 4(x + 5)$
g) $10x^2(4x + 3) - 6x(2x - 1)$ **h)** $(4x + 2)(3x + 2)$ **i)** $(5x + 6)(5x - 6)$ **j)** $(4x^2 + 3x)(2x + 2)$ **k)** $(2x^3 - 3)(4 - 3x^2)$

4 Factorise the following expressions:
a) $9x - 15$ **b)** $9x + 9$ **c)** $20x^2 - x$ **d)** $4x - 20x^3$ **e)** $20x^2y^2 + 36xy$ **f)** $4(3x - 5) + y(3x - 5)$

5 **a)** Expand and simplify $(a + b)^2$ **b)** Without using a calculator, work out the value of $8.8^2 + 2 \times 8.8 \times 1.2 + 1.2^2$

Linear Equations

1 Solve the following equations:

a) $5x = 35$

b) $3x + 4 = 16$

c) $5x + 8 = 23$

d) $2(x + 2) = 12$

e) $5(x - 3) = 10$

f) $4(5 + 3x) = 14$

g) $\frac{x}{3} = 6$

h) $\frac{x}{2} + \frac{x}{6} = 10$

i) $\frac{x + 2}{5} = 3$

j) $5x = 2x + 9$

k) $7x = 15 - 3x$

l) $2x = x - 8$

m) $11x + 3 = 3x + 7$

n) $5 + 7x = 23 + 3x$

o) $10x - 6 = 3x + 15$

p) $8(3x - 2) = 20$

q) $5(x + 7) = 3(9 + x)$

r) $8(4x - 6) = 7(3x - 10)$

s) $\frac{5x + 4}{3} + \frac{8 - x}{2} = 10$

t) $\frac{9x + 10}{4} - \frac{4x - 4}{10} = 14$

u) $\frac{2x + 6}{5} = x - 3$

Linear Equations

2 **Maggie is *x* years old.**   **Nigel is twice Maggie's age.**   **Helen is 4 years older than Nigel.**

a) Write down an expression in terms of *x* for their combined age.

....

....

b) Their total combined age is 64 years. Write an equation for their ages and solve it to find Helen's age.

....

....

3 **ABC is a triangle:**

a) Write down an expression in terms of *x* for the perimeter of the triangle.

....

b) The perimeter of triangle ABC is 50cm. Form an equation and solve it to find *x*.

....

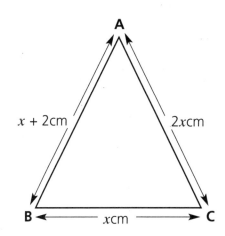

$x + 2$cm $2x$cm

B ◄——— $x$cm ———► C

4 **ABCD is a rectangle:**

a) Write down an expression in terms of *x* for the area of the rectangle.

....

b) The area of rectangle ABCD is 72cm². Form an equation and solve it to find *x*.

....

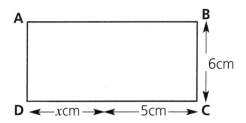

A   B

6cm

D ◄—$x$cm—►◄—5cm—► C

---

5 **Solve the following equations to find the value of *x*:**

a) $2x + 5 = 17$ **b)** $15 + 3x = 3$ **c)** $4x = x + 18$ **d)** $10x = 7x - 15$ **e)** $4x - 3 = 6x + 12$ **f)** $9x + 7 = 4x - 13$

g) $14 + 5x = 7x + 2$ **h)** $23 - 8x = x - 4$ **i)** $40x - 36 = 7x + 30$ **j)** $4(x + 5) = 36$ **k)** $7(2x - 3) = 14$ **l)** $6 = 4(3x - 9)$

m) $16 = 4(11 - 5x)$ **n)** $5(x + 1) = 2(x + 7)$ **o)** $11(3x + 2) = (6x - 5)$ **p)** $9(2x + 4) - 4(5x + 8) = 0$

q) $\dfrac{x - 10}{10} + \dfrac{2x + 1}{5} = 0.7$ **r)** $\dfrac{4x + 6}{2} - \dfrac{10x}{15} = 5$

6 **For each of the following, derive an equation and solve it to find *x*.**

a)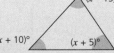

$(x - 15)°$

$(x + 10)°$ $(x + 5)°$

b)

$(3x + 20)°$ $(5x - 5)°$

$4x°$ $(5x + 5)°$

c)

$\dfrac{5x°}{3}$

$3x°$ $(2x + 20)°$

Formulae

1 **Rearrange the following formulae to make x the subject:**

a) $x + 4y = 3$

b) $6x + 7y = 50$

c) $7x - 5 = 3y$

d) $\dfrac{x}{y} + 5 = z$

e) $\dfrac{x + 3y}{4} = 5$

f) $\dfrac{4x - 3}{y} = 8$

g) $5x + 3y = 3(6 - x)$

h) $4x^2 = 3y$

i) $\dfrac{x^2}{y} = 6y$

j) $5x^2 + 3 = 7y$

k) $xd^2 = \dfrac{b}{c} - x$

l) $tx = \sqrt{m + x^2}$

2 **The volume of a cone is given by the formula:** $V = \frac{1}{3}\pi r^2 h$

Calculate the volume of a cone in cm^3 if r = 4cm, h = 10cm and π = 3.

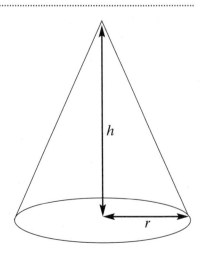

Formulae

xy

3 The distance travelled (s) by an object depends on its initial speed (u), its final speed (v) and the time of travel (t). It is given by the formula: $s = \left(\dfrac{u + v}{2}\right)t$

Calculate the distance travelled in metres if initial speed = 4m/s, final speed = 12m/s and time = 5.5s

....

....

....

4 The formula that converts a temperature reading from degrees Celsius (°C) into degrees Fahrenheit (°F) is: $F = \dfrac{9}{5} C + 32$

What is the temperature in degrees Celsius if the temperature in degrees Fahrenheit is 212°F?

....

....

....

5 The circumference of a circle is given by the formula $C = 2\pi r$, where r is the radius.

The area of a circle is given by the formula $A = \pi r^2$.

a) Write a formula for the area of a circle in terms of its circumference, C.

....

....

b) Use your formula to work out the area of a circle in cm^2, which has a circumference of 40cm.

Use $\pi = 3.14$. Give your answer to 2 significant figures.

....

....

....

6 Rearrange the following formulae to make p the subject:
a) $4p - 3 = 4q$ **b)** $4 - 6p = q$ **c)** $3(2p + 5) = 4p + 11q$ **d)** $3p^2 + 4 = 8q$ **e)** $\dfrac{3p^2 - 6}{4} = 2q$

7 The area of a parallelogram is given by the formula: Area = length × height. Calculate the area, in m^2, of a parallelogram that has length = 90cm and height = 1.2m.

8 The area, A, of a circle is given by the formula: $A = \pi r^2$, where r is the radius. Calculate the radius if area = 100cm^2 and $\pi = 3.14$ Give your answer to 2 significant figures.

9 **a)** Make l the subject of the formula $T = 2\pi \sqrt{\left(\dfrac{l}{g}\right)}$ **b)** Calculate l to 3 s.f given that $T = 1$ and $g = 9.81$

Quadratic Expressions

1 **Factorise the following quadratic expressions:**

a) $x^2 + 6x + 8$

b) $x^2 + 7x + 10$

c) $x^2 + 9x - 10$

d) $x^2 + 8x - 20$

e) $x^2 - 100$

f) $x^2 - 144$

2 **Factorise the following quadratic expressions:**

a) $2x^2 + 5x - 3$

b) $4x^2 + 3x - 1$

c) $2x^2 + 7x + 3$

d) $6x^2 + x - 2$

e) $6y^2 - 11y - 10$

f) $12n^2 - 11n + 2$

3 **Rearrange the expression $3 - 5x - 2x^2$ then factorise.**

4 **Factorise the following quadratic expressions:**
a) $x^2 + 5x + 6$ b) $x^2 - 5x + 6$ c) $x^2 + 5x - 6$ d) $x^2 - 5x - 6$
e) $x^2 + x - 30$ f) $x^2 + 31x + 30$ g) $x^2 - 81$ h) $x^2 - 169$

5 **Rearrange the following expressions where necessary then factorise completely:**
a) $42 - 34n + 4n^2$ b) $25y^2 + 4 - 20y$ c) $11x - 6x^2 - 3$

6 a) Factorise $7n^2 + 52n + 21$
b) Use your result from part a) to write 75 221 as a product of two 3-digit numbers. Explain your reasoning.
c) The number 32 207 is the product of two 3-digit numbers. What expression could you factorise to find these 3-digit numbers?

Quadratic Equations

xy

1 **Factorise these quadratic equations and then solve them.**

a) $a^2 + a - 6 = 0$

b) $a^2 + 4a - 5 = 0$

c) $a^2 - 2a - 8 = 0$

d) $2a^2 - 5a - 3 = 0$

e) $3a^2 + 14a + 8 = 0$

f) $8a^2 + 6a - 9 = 0$

2 **Solve these equations, rearranging them first.**

a) $x^2 + 5x = 6$

b) $x^2 + 28 = 11x$

c) $x^2 - 3x + 3 = 1$

3 **A rectangle has dimensions as shown in the diagram opposite. The area of the rectangle is 80cm².**

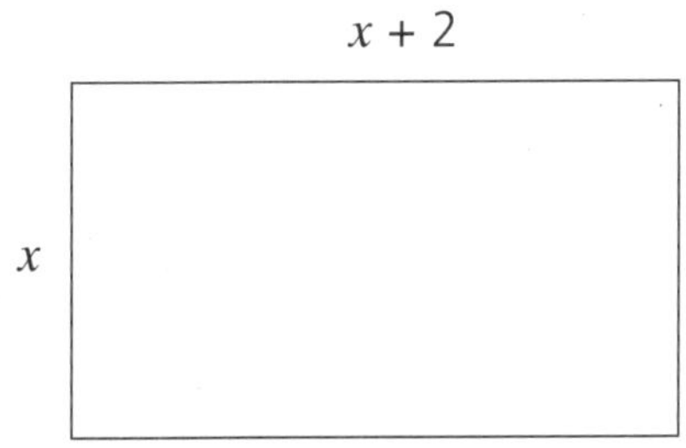

$x + 2$

x

a) Write an equation for the area.

b) Solve this equation.

c) Find the perimeter of the rectangle. ....

4 **The squares of two consecutive whole numbers add up to 61. Let n be the first number.**

a) Write an expression for the second number. ....

b) Write an equation for the sum of the squares of the two consecutive numbers.

c) Solve the equation to find the two whole numbers.

Quadratic Equations

1 **Find the solutions of these equations (to 2 d.p.) by completing the square.**

a) $x^2 + 10x - 4 = 0$ **b)** $x^2 - 10x + 1 = 0$ **c)** $x^2 - 4x - 3 = 0$

2 **Annika's vegetable plot has the dimensions shown in the diagram. She decides to increase the size of the plot by adding x metres to the length and width.**

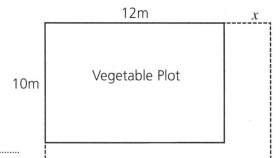

a) Write down an expression for the area of the entire enlarged plot, multiplying out any brackets.

b) Write an expression for the area of the extension only.

c) Find x if Annika increases the area by 104m^2.

---

3 **Solve these equations by either factorising or completing the square.**
a) $x^2 - 7x + 3 = 0$ **b)** $4a^2 - 19a + 12 = 0$ **c)** $x^2 - x - 6 = 14$ **d)** $x^2 + 12x - 5 = 0$
e) $35 - 2a = a^2$ **f)** $4y^2 - 8y + 3 = 0$

4 **The difference between the square of a number and the number itself is 72. Write down and solve an equation to find the two possible values of the number.**

5 **The sum of the first n numbers in the sequence '1, 2, 3, 4…' is given by the formula $\frac{n}{2}(n + 1)$. How many numbers must be added to give a sum of 55?**

Quadratic Equations

1 Find the solutions to these quadratic equations (to 2 d.p.) using the quadratic formula. You may need to rearrange them first.

a) $2x^2 + 3x - 1 = 0$

b) $2 - 3x - x^2 = 0$

c) $5x^2 + 4x = 2$

2 In the triangle opposite AC is 2m shorter than AB.

a) Using Pythagoras' theorem write down an equation for x.

b) Show how this can be simplified to $x^2 - 2x - 70 = 0$

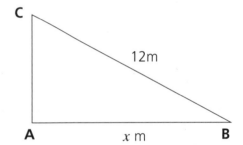

c) Solve this equation using the quadratic formula.

3 Solve these equations to 1 d.p. using the quadratic formula.
a) $x(x + 2) = 5$ **b)** $x^2 = 4x - 3$ **c)** $(x + 1)(x - 2) = 3$
d) $x^2 + 10x - 4 = 0$ **e)** $3x^2 - 3x = 2$ **f)** $4 - 5x - x^2 = 0$

4 A square picture with sides of 20cm is put in a frame w cm wide.
a) Write an expression for the area of the frame in terms of w.
b) If the picture has an area of half the area of the frame and picture together, write an equation for w.
c) Show that this equation can be simplified to $w^2 + 20w - 100 = 0$
d) Solve the equation to find the width of the frame (w) to 1 d.p.

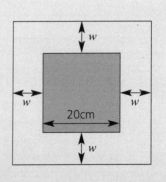

Trial and Improvement

1 The equation $x^3 - x = 15$ has a solution that lies between 2 and 3. By trial and improvement calculate a solution to 1 d.p.

x	$x^3 - x$	Comment
2	$2^3 - 2 = 8 - 2 = 6$	Less than 15
3	$3^3 - 3 = 27 - 3 = 24$	More than 15

Answer: ....

2 The equation $x^3 + 2x = 40$ has a solution that lies between 3 and 4. By trial and improvement calculate a solution to 2 d.p.

x	$x^3 + 2x$	Comment

Answer: ....

3 A rectangular box has the following dimensions:

a) Show that the volume of the box is given by the expression $x^3 + 3x^2$.

....

b) The volume of the box is 40cm³. Using trial and improvement, find x which has a value that lies between 2 and 3. Give your answer to 1 d.p.

x	$x^3 + 3x^2$	Comment

Answer: ....

4 **a)** The equation $x^3 + 10x = 24$ has one solution that lies between 1 and 2. Using trial and improvement, find the solution to 1 decimal place.

b) The equation $x^3 - 6x = 65$ has one solution that lies between 4 and 5. Using trial and improvement, find the solution to 2 decimal places.

5 A rectangular box has the following dimensions: length = $2x$ cm, width = x cm and height = $x + 3$cm.

a) Show that the volume of the box is given by the expression $2x^3 + 6x^2$.

b) The volume of the box is 50cm³. Using trial and improvement, find x which has a value that lies between 2 and 3. Give your answer to 1 decimal place.

Sequences

$$xy$$

1 **a)** The first four numbers of a sequence are: 1, 3, 7, 15…

The rule to continue this sequence of numbers is:

Multiply the previous number by 2 and then add 1

i) What are the next two numbers in the sequence? ....

ii) The following sequence obeys the same rule: -2, -3, -5, -9…

What are the next two numbers in this sequence? ....

b) The first four numbers of a sequence are: 3, 4, 6, 10…

The rule to continue this sequence of numbers is:

Subtract 1 from the previous number and then multiply by 2

i) What are the next two numbers in the sequence? ....

ii) The following sequence obeys the same rule: 1, 0, -2, -6…

What are the next two numbers in this sequence? ....

2 **a)** The first four square numbers are 1, 4, 9 and 16. What are the next four numbers in the sequence?

....

b) The first four triangular numbers are 1, 3, 6 and 10. What are the next four numbers in the sequence?

....

3 The nth term of a sequence is $5n + 8$.

a) What is the value of the 3rd term? | **b)** What is the value of the 10th term?

.... | ....

4 The nth term of a sequence is $2n - 11$.

a) What is the value of the 4th term? | **b)** What is the value of the 16th term?

.... | ....

5 The nth term of a sequence is $2n - 9$.

a) Which term has a value of 19? | **b)** Which term has a value of -5?

.... | ....

6 The nth term of a sequence is $7n + 6$.

a) Which term has a value of 69? | **b)** Which term has a value of 90?

.... | ....

7 nth term is $50 - 3n$.

a) What is the value of the 7th term? | **b)** What is the value of the 22nd term?

.... | ....

c) Which term has a value of 11? | **d)** Which term's value is -7?

.... | ....

Sequences

7 The first four terms of a sequence are: **3, 5, 7, 9...**

Write down a formula for the nth term of this sequence and add a further 5 terms to the sequence.

....

....

8 The first four terms of a sequence are: **6, 4, 2, 0...**

Write down a formula for the nth term of this sequence and add a further 5 terms to the sequence.

....

....

9 Here is a sequence of diagrams made up of squares:

Diagram 1   **Diagram 2**   **Diagram 3**   **Diagram 4**

a) Write down a formula for the number of squares (s) in terms of diagram number (n).

....

....

....

b) How many squares would there be in diagram 8?

....

c) Which number diagram would have 49 squares?

....

10 Here is a sequence of diagrams made up of circles:

Diagram 1   **Diagram 2**   **Diagram 3**   **Diagram 4**

a) Write down a formula for the number of circles (c) in terms of diagram number (n).

....

....

b) How many circles would there be in diagram 15?

....

c) Which number diagram would have 81 circles?

....

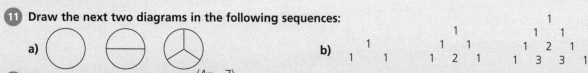

11 Draw the next two diagrams in the following sequences:

a)

b)

```
                              1
              1             1   1
      1     1   1         1   2   1
  1       1   2   1     1   3   3   1
```

12 The nth term of a sequence is $\dfrac{(4n-7)}{3}$ **a)** What is the value of the 10th term?   **b)** Which term has a value of 27?

13 The first four terms of a sequence are: 15, 11, 7, 3...

a) Write down a formula for the nth term of this sequence.   **b)** What is the value of **i)** the 10th term? **ii)** the 100th term?

Straight Line Graphs

xy

1 **On the axes provided, draw and label the graphs of the following linear functions for values of x between -2 and 2:**

a) $y = 2x - 1$

x	-2	0	2
y	-5		

b) $y = x + 2$

x			
y			

c) $y = -2x$

x			
y			

d) $y = -x - 3$

x			
y			

e) $y = \frac{1}{2}x + 3$

x			
y			

2 **a)** Make y the subject of the following function:

$2y - x = 8$

....

....

b) On the axes below, draw and label the graph of the rearranged function from part **a)**.

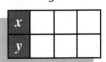

x			
y			

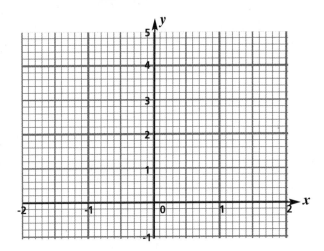

c) A point, which lies on the line of the graph that you have just drawn, has the coordinates $(5, p)$. Calculate the value of p.

....

....

d) Another point that lies on the line of the drawn graph has the coordinates $(q, 0)$. Calculate the value of q.

....

....

3 **a)** Make y the subject of the following function: $y - 3x = -4$
b) Draw the graph of the rearranged function for values of x between -3 and 3.
c) Use the graph to calculate the value of y if $x = 1.5$
d) Use the graph to calculate the value of x if $y = 3.2$

4 **a)** Draw graphs of $y = 3x$ and $y = x + 5$ for values of x between 0 and 4 on the same set of axes.
b) What is the x coordinate of the point where the two lines cross?
c) Now solve the equation $3x = x + 5$.

Gradients

1 **Find the gradient and intercept of the following linear functions:**

a) $y = 2x + 1$

....

....

....

b) $y = 5 - 3x$

....

....

....

c) $x + y = 3$

....

....

....

d) $4y = 7 - 8x$

....

....

....

e) $2y - 2x = 9$

....

....

....

f) $2x = y - 2$

....

....

....

2 **Four of the equations from question 1 have been plotted below. What is the equation of each line?**

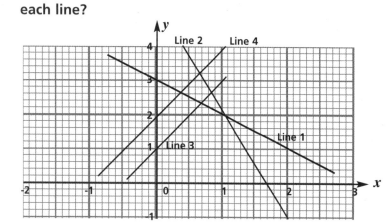

Line 1: ....

Line 2: ....

Line 3: ....

Line 4: ....

3 **What is the equation of the line that crosses the *y*-axis at…**

a) (0,1) and is parallel to $y = 2x$? ....

b) (0,1) and is parallel to $y = -2x$? ....

c) (0,-2) and is parallel to $y = 2x$? ....

d) (0,-2) and is parallel to $y = x + 2$? ....

e) (0,3) and is perpendicular to $y = -x - 3$? ....

f) (0,-3.5) and is perpendicular to $y = -x$? ....

---

4 **Find the gradient and intercept of the following linear functions:**
a) $y = -3x - 3$ **b)** $4y = 3x + 8$ **c)** $2y - x = 3$ **d)** $x - 2y = 3$ **e)** $2y - 3 = x$ **f)** $\dfrac{y - 2x}{3} = 5$ **g)** $\dfrac{y - 4x}{5} = 1$

5 **What is the equation of the line that crosses the *y*-axis at a)** (0,4) and is parallel to $y = x - 4$ **b)** (0,0) and is perpendicular to $y = x - 4$

6 **Which of the following linear functions would produce parallel lines if drawn on the same axes?**
i) $y = 2x + 3$ **ii)** $y + 2x = 3$ **iii)** $2y - 4x = 7$ **iv)** $y - 6 = 2x$

7 **Which of the following linear functions would produce perpendicular lines if drawn on the same axes?**
i) $y - 2x = 4$ **ii)** $3x + y = 7$ **iii)** $3y - x = 4$ **iv)** $3y + 3x = 5$

Linear Inequalities

xy

1 Solve the following inequalities and complete the number line for each one:

a) $x + 2 > 11$ ....

b) $8 > x - 9$ ....

c) $2x + 5 \leqslant 15$ 41

d) $13 \geqslant 5 + 4x$ ....

e) $7x - 2 \leqslant 2x + 13$ ....

f) $6 + 3x < 21 - 2x$ ....

2 Solve the following inequalities:

a) $12 + 3x < 6$

b) $14 > 5 - 3x$

c) $5(4x + 7) \geqslant 15$

d) $3(2x + 5) \geqslant 24$

e) $6(4 - x) \leqslant 9$

f) $8 \geqslant 3 - 2x$

3 Draw, label and shade the region represented by each inequality on the grids provided.

a) $x \geqslant 1$

b) $y < -2$

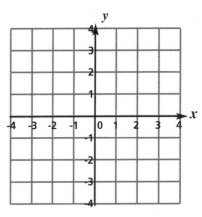

c) $y > -x + 2$

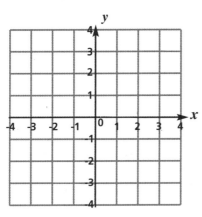

d) $y \leqslant 2x - 1$

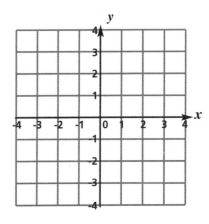

Linear Inequalities

4 a) On the grid, draw and shade the region that satisfies these three inequalities:

$x \leqslant 3$, $y \leqslant 4$ and $x + y \geqslant 4$

Label the region A.

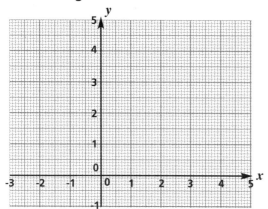

b) B is a point within region A, and has coordinates that are both integers.

What are the coordinates of B?

....

5 a) On the grid, draw and shade the region that satisfies these three inequalities:

$x < 4$, $y \geqslant 1$ and $x > y$

Label the region A.

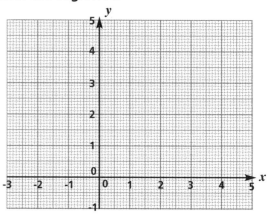

b) B is a point within region A, and has coordinates that are both integers.

What are the coordinates of B?

....

6 On the grid, draw and shade the region that satisfies these four inequalities:

$x > -2$, $y \geqslant 0$, $y \geqslant 0.5x$, $x + y < 3$

Label the region A.

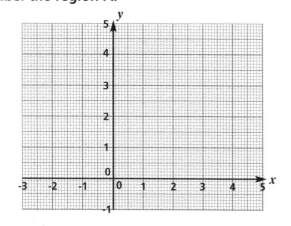

7 On the grid, the region labelled A satisfies four inequalities, what are they?

....

....

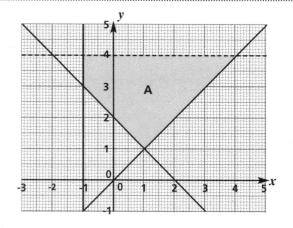

8 Solve the following inequalities and for each one draw a number line. **a)** $4x \geqslant 20$ **b)** $x + 3 > 5$ **c)** $4x - 3 \leqslant 19$ **d)** $8x + 5 < 2x - 7$ **e)** $5(2x - 3) < 4x + 9$ **f)** $7(3x - 2) \geqslant 20x - 16$ **g)** $6(3x - 2) < 4(4x - 10)$

9 On a suitable grid, draw and shade the region that satisfies these three inequalities: $x \geqslant 2$, $y \leqslant 5$ and $y \geqslant x$. Label the region A.

10 On a suitable grid, draw and shade the region that satisfies these four inequalities: $x > -1$, $y \geqslant x - 2$, $y > -1$ and $y \leqslant -x + 5$. Label the region A.

Simultaneous Equations

xy

1 Solve the following simultaneous equations:

a) $2x + y = 8$

   $x + y = 5$

....

....

....

....

....

....

b) $2x + 5y = 24$

   $3x - 5y = 11$

....

....

....

....

....

....

c) $x - 6y = 17$

   $3x + 2y = 11$

....

....

....

....

....

....

d) $4x + 3y = 27$

   $x + y = 7$

....

....

....

....

....

....

....

e) $5x - 2y = 14$

   $2x + 3y = 17$

....

....

....

....

....

....

....

f) $3x + 4y = 13$

   $2x - 3y = 3$

....

....

....

....

....

....

....

2 At break time a student buys two doughnuts and a coffee, which costs her 84p altogether. At lunchtime, the same student buys three doughnuts and two coffees, which cost 138p altogether. Form two equations with the information given and work out the individual price of a doughnut (*d*) and a coffee (*c*).

....

....

....

....

....

3 Solve the following simultaneous equations:
   a) $5x + y = 14$, $3x + y = 10$ **b)** $4x - y = 6$, $x + y = 9$ **c)** $3x + 2y = 8$, $x + y = 2$ **d)** $4x + 6y = 12$, $x + y = 1$
   e) $4x + 2y = 13$, $10x - 4y = 1$ **f)** $x - 10y = 2$, $4x + 2y = -13$ **g)** $4x - 3y = -6$, $y - 3x = 7$ **h)** $10x + 2y = 0$, $x - y = 9$

Simultaneous Equations

1 a) On the axes opposite, draw and label the graph of the following equations:

$y = x + 8$ and $y = 2x + 5$

x	0	2	4	x	0	2	4
$y = x + 8$	8	10	12	$y = 2x + 5$	5	9	13

b) Use your graph to solve the simultaneous equations: $y = x + 8$ and $y = 2x + 5$

....

2 a) Complete the table, then on the axes opposite, draw and label the graph of the following equations:

$y = 3x + 10$ and $y = -x + 22$

x	0	2	4	x	0	2	4
$y = 3x + 10$				$y = -x + 22$			

b) Use your graph to solve the simultaneous equations: $y = 3x + 10$ and $y = -x + 22$

....

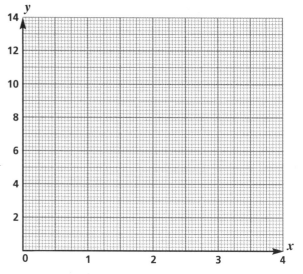

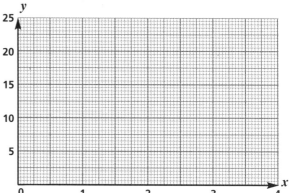

3 a) On the axes opposite, draw the graphs of the following lines:

i) $y = -x + 4$

ii) $y = x + 2$

iii) $y = -0.25x + 1$

b) Use your graph to solve the following simultaneous equations:

i) $y = x + 2$ and $y = -0.25x + 1$ ....

ii) $y = x + 2$ and $y = -x + 4$ ....

iii) $y = -x + 4$ and $y = -0.25x + 1$ ....

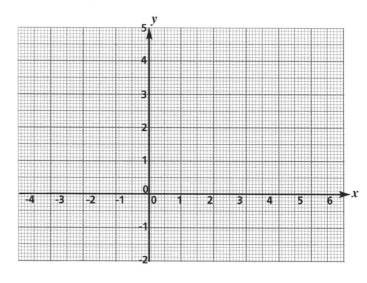

4 a) Draw the graph of $2x + y = 13$ and $3x = y - 3$ for values of x between 0 and 4.
b) Use your graph to solve the simultaneous equations: $2x + y = 13$ and $3x = y - 3$.

5 a) Draw the graph of $x + y = 6$, $3x - y = 2$ and $x - y = 4$ for values of x between -2 and 6.
b) Use your graph to solve the following simultaneous equations: **i)** $x + y = 6$, $3x - y = 2$ **ii)** $x + y = 6$, $x - y = 4$
iii) $3x - y = 2$, $x - y = 4$

Simultaneous Equations

xy

1 **Solve these simultaneous equations (to 1 d.p.)**

a) $y = 3 - 14x$ and $y = 5x^2$

b) $y = 10x^2$ and $y = x + 24$

2 **Solve these simultaneous equations by substitution. If need be give your answers to 2 d.p.**

a) $x^2 + y^2 = 1$ and $x + y = 1$

b) $x^2 + y^2 = 9$ and $x + y = 2$

Simultaneous Equations

1 **a)** Using the axes opposite, solve graphically the simultaneous equations $y - x = 1$ and $y = x^2$

....

....

....

b) Check your answers to part **a)** by solving the simultaneous equations by substitution.

....

....

....

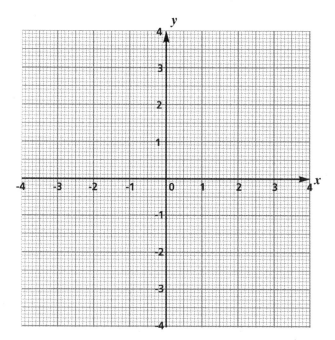

2 **Using the axes opposite, solve graphically these pairs of simultaneous equations:**

a) $x^2 + y^2 = 9$

  $y - x = 2$

b) $x^2 + y^2 = 9$

  $x + y = 2$

....

....

....

3 **Solve these simultaneous equations: a)** by substitution **b)** graphically. (If need be, give your answer to 1 d.p.)

  i) $y = 2x^2$ **ii)** $y = \frac{1}{2}x^2$ **iii)** $y = x^2$

    $y - x = 2$ $x + y = 1$ $x + y = 1$

4 **Solve graphically the following simultaneous equations:**

  a) $x^2 + y^2 = 4$ **b)** $x^2 + y^2 = 9$ **c)** $x^2 + y^2 = 1$

    $y = 2x$ $y = -x + 2$ $y = \frac{1}{2}x^2$

Graphs of Quadratic Functions

1 Below is a table of values for $y = x^2 - 2$

x	-2	-1	0	1	2
y	2	-1	-2	-1	2

a) Draw the graph of $y = x^2 - 2$

b) From your graph find the value(s) of…

i) y when $x = 1.5$

....

ii) x when $y = 1.5$

....

2 Below is an incomplete table of values for

$y = 2x^2 + x - 5$

a) Complete the table.

x	-3	-2	-1	0	1	2
$2x^2$		8		0		8
$+x$		-2		0		2
-5		-5		-5		-5
$y = 2x^2 + x - 5$		1		-5		5

b) Draw the graph of $y = 2x^2 + x - 5$

c) From your graph find the value(s) of…

i) y when $x = -2.5$

....

ii) x when $y = 1.6$

....

d) From your graph find the solution to the

equation $2x^2 + x - 5 = 0$

....

e) From your graph find the solution to the

equation $2x^2 + x - 5 = 1$

....

f) From your graph find the solution to the

equation $2x^2 + x - 5 = -2$

....

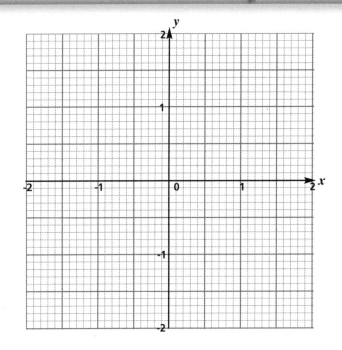

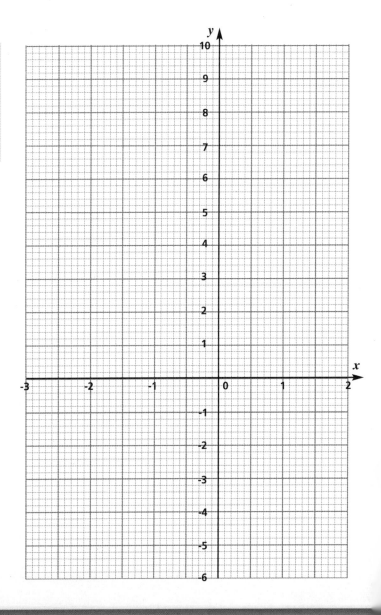

Graphs of Quadratic Functions

3 **Below is an incomplete table of values for** $y = x^2 + 2x - 4$.

x	-4	-3	-2	-1	0	1	2
x^2		9		1		1	
$+2x$		-6		-2		2	
-4		-4		-4		-4	
$y = x^2 + 2x - 4$		-1		-5		-1	

a) Complete the table.

b) Draw the graph of $y = x^2 + 2x - 4$

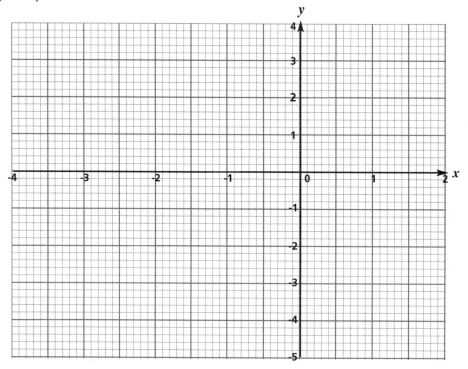

c) From your graph find the solutions to the following equations:

i) $x^2 + 2x - 4 = 0$ **ii)** $x^2 + 2x - 6 = 0$ **iii)** $x^2 + 2x = 1$

....

....

....

---

4 **a)** Draw a table of results for $y = 10 - x^2$ for values of x between -4 and 4.
b) Draw the graph of $y = 10 - x^2$.
c) From your graph find the solutions to the equations: **i)** $10 - x^2 = 0$ **ii)** $10 - x^2 = 6$ **iii)** $10 - x^2 = -2$

5 **a)** Draw the graph of $y = x^2 - 12$ for values of x between -4 and 4.
b) From your graph find the solutions to the equations: **i)** $x^2 - 12 = 0$ **ii)** $x^2 = 15$ **iii)** $x^2 - 6 = 0$

Graphs of Other Functions

1 **Below is an incomplete table of values for** $y = x^3 + 10$

a) Complete the table.

x	-3	-2	-1	0	1	2
x^3		-8		0		8
+10		+10		+10		+10
$y = x^3 + 10$		2		10		18

b) On the axes opposite draw the graph of

$y = x^3 + 10$

c) Use your graph to find...

   i) the value of x when $y = -10$

   ....

   ii) the value of y when $x = 1.5$

   ....

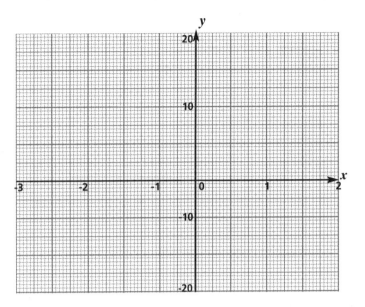

2 **Below is a table of values for**

$y = \frac{1}{x}$ **with** $x \neq 0$

x	-5	-4	-3	-2	-1	-0.5	-0.3̇	-0.25	-0.2
$y = \frac{1}{x}$	-0.2	-0.25	-0.3̇	-0.5	-1	-2	-3	-4	-5

x	0.2	0.25	0.3̇	0.5	1	2	3	4	5
$y = \frac{1}{x}$	5	4	3	2	1	0.5	0.3̇	0.25	0.2

a) On the axes opposite draw the graph

of $y = \frac{1}{x}$ with $x \neq 0$

b) Use your graph to find...

   i) the value of x when $y = 2.5$ ....

   ii) the value of y when $x = -1.5$ ....

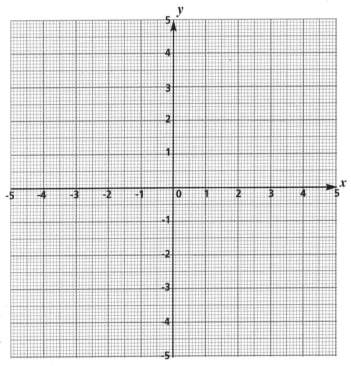

3 **Below is an incomplete table of values for** $y = x^3 - 2$

x	-3	-2	-1	0	1	2	3
x^3		-8		0		8	
-2		-2		-2		-2	
$y = x^3 - 2$		-10		-2		6	

a) Complete the table.

b) Draw the graph of $y = x^3 - 2$.

c) Use your graph to find the value of x when $y = 0$

d) Use your graph to find...

   i) the value of x when $y = 20$

   ii) the value of y when $x = 1.5$

Graphs of Other Functions

1 **a)** For values of x from -2 to 2 complete the tables below.

x	-2	-1	0	1	2
4^x					

x	-2	-1	0	1	2
$\left(\frac{1}{4}\right)^x$					

b) Draw graphs of $y = 4^x$ and $y = \left(\frac{1}{4}\right)^x$ on the same axes opposite.

c) What do you notice about the graphs of the two functions?

....

....

....

....

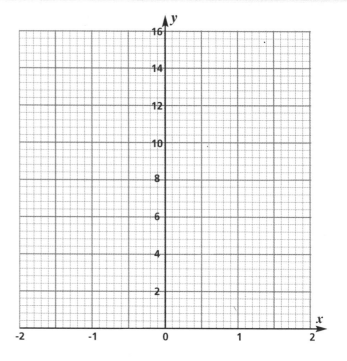

2 **The table below shows values of x and y for the relationship $y = ab^x$**

x	0	1	2	3
y	10	20	40	80

a) Using the axes opposite draw the graph of the relationship $y = ab^x$

b) Use the graph to find the values of a and b and the relationship.

....

....

....

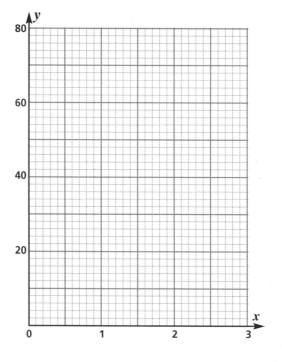

3 Draw the graphs of the following exponential functions for values of x from 0 to 4
a) $y = 4^x$ **b)** $y = 3 \times 0.5^x$ **c)** $y = -1 \times 2^x$

4 A graph fits the relationship $y = ab^x$. When $x = 0$, $y = 2$ and when $x = 2$, $y = 18$.
a) Find the values of a and b and hence the relationship.
b) Draw the graph of this relationship.

Graphs of Other Functions

xy

1 **a)** Complete this table of values for the graph of $y = \sin x$

$x(°)$	0	30	60	90	120	150	180	210	240	270	300	330	360
$y = \sin x$													

b) On the grid opposite carefully plot the points and draw the graph of $y = \sin x$.

c) Use your graph to estimate two angles that have $\sin x = 0.8$

....

....

....

d) Use your graph to estimate $\sin 45°$.

....

....

....

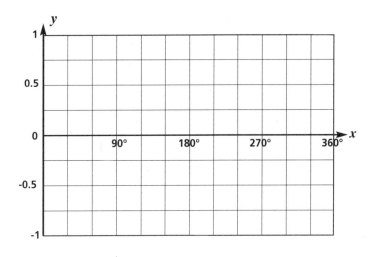

2 **a)** Complete this table of values for the graph of $y = \cos x$

$x(°)$	0	30	60	90	120	150	180	210	240	270	300	330	360
$y = \cos x$													

b) On the grid opposite carefully plot the points and draw the graph of $y = \cos x$

c) Use your graph to estimate two angles that have $\cos x = 0.6$

....

....

....

d) Use your graph to estimate $\cos 315°$.

....

....

....

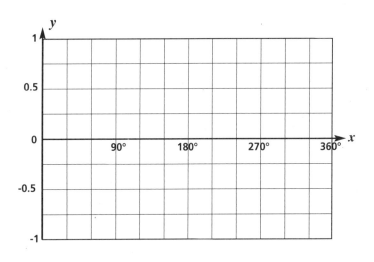

3 **a)** On a suitable grid draw the graph of $y = \tan x$ for values of x from 0° to 360°.

b) In which ways is the graph of $y = \tan x$ similar and different to the graphs of $y = \sin x$ and $y = \cos x$? (see question **1** + **2**)

Transformation of Functions

1 **a)** On the axes opposite draw and label the graph of $y = x^2$ for values of x from -3 to 3

b) On the same axes, sketch and label the graphs of...

i) $y = x^2 - 4$

ii) $y = 3x^2$

c) **i)** Describe fully the transformation that maps $y = x^2$ onto $y = x^2 - 4$

....

....

....

ii) Describe fully the transformation that maps $y = x^2$ onto $y = 3x^2$

....

....

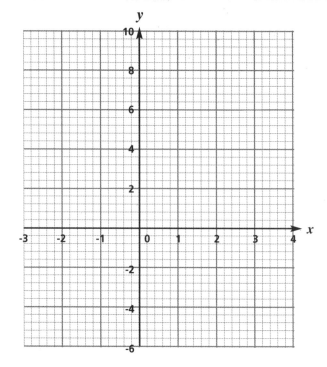

2 **a)** On the axes below sketch the graphs of **i)** $y = \sin x$ **ii)** $y = \frac{1}{2}\sin x$ **iii)** $y = \sin 2x$

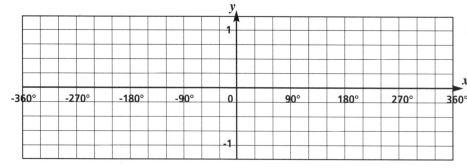

b) Describe the transformation that maps $y = \sin x$ onto...

i) $y = \frac{1}{2}\sin x$ ....

....

ii) $y = \sin 2x$ ....

....

3 **a)** On the axes opposite sketch the graphs of **i)** $y = \cos x$

ii) $y = \cos(x + 90°)$ **iii)** $y = \cos x - 1$

b) Describe the transformation that maps $y = \cos x$ onto...

i) $y = \cos(x + 90°)$ ....

ii) $y = \cos x - 1$ ....

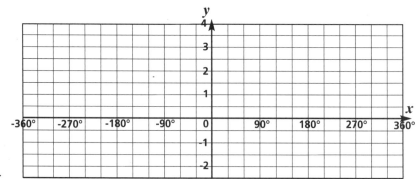

4 **Sketch these graphs on the same axes:**
a) $y = x^2$ $y = 4x^2$ $y = x^2 - 1$ **b)** $y = x^2$ $y = (3x)^2$ $y = (x + 5)^2$ **c)** $y = x^2$ $y = \frac{1}{3}x^2$ $y = x^2 + 3$

5 **a)** On a suitable set of axes sketch the graphs of $y = \cos x$, $y = 3\cos x$, $y = \cos x + 3$
b) On a suitable set of axes sketch the graphs of $y = \sin x$, $y = \sin\frac{1}{2}x$, $y = \sin(x + 45°)$

6 Sketch these graphs on the same axes:
a) $y = -x^2$ **b)** $y = -2x^2$ $y = -x^2 + 2$

Real Life Graphs

1. **Two towns A and B are 100 miles apart. Mr Brown lives in A and drives to B and Mr Smith lives in B and drives to A on the same day, along the same route. Using the graph opposite…**

   a) What time did Mr Smith set off? ....

   b) Which motorist completed the journey in
      the shortest time? ....

   c) Who reached the highest speed and what was it? ....

   d) What happened at Y? ....

   e) Who stopped and for how long? ....

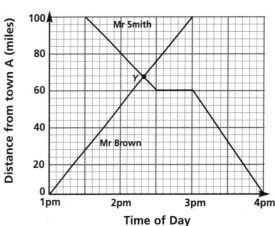

2. **The sketch graphs opposite show the cost of running a business over several months. Identify which sketch matches each of these descriptions.**

   a) Costs are rising steadily. ....

   b) Costs are falling after reaching a peak. ....

   c) Costs are rising at an increasing rate. ....

   d) Costs have been rising but are now levelling out. ....

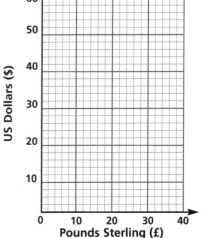

3. **a)** If £1 = $1.4 complete the table to convert pounds
      sterling (£) to US dollars ($).

Pounds (£)	10	20	30	40
US Dollars ($)				

   b) On the axes opposite draw the graph to
      convert pounds (£) to US dollars ($).

   c) Use your graph to convert $30 into pounds. ....

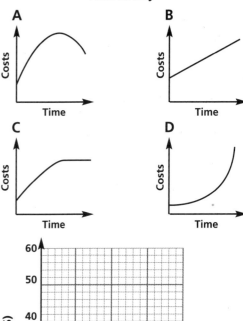

4. **Three plumbers A, B and C charge as follows: A – Call out charge £20 then £10 per hour extra. B – Call out charge £30 then £5 per hour extra. C – Standard charge £50 regardless of time.**

   a) Draw a graph for each plumber's charges on the same axes, for up to 5 hours work.

   b) Which plumber is cheapest for a 30 minute job?

   c) Which plumber is cheapest for a $2\frac{1}{2}$ hour job?

   d) After what time will plumber C become the cheapest?

5. **A tank of water, cuboid in shape, is being drained out at a rate of 10cm depth per minute. If the water is 60cm deep to start with, draw a graph of time against depth.**

Direct and Inverse Proportion

1 The table below gives the number of bacteria, N, in a culture at hourly intervals. The number of bacteria is directly proportional to the time, t (hours).

t (hours)	0	1	2	3	4	5
N (bacteria)	0	10	20	30	40	50

a) Draw the graph of N against t on the axes opposite.

b) What is the relationship (algebraic rule) between N and t?

....

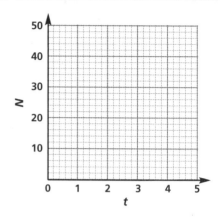

2 The weight, W (kg), of a metal bar is directly proportional to the square of its diameter, d (cm), when the length of the bar is constant.

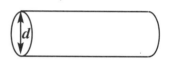

a) Complete the table below.

d^2	0					
d	0	1	2	3	4	5
W	0	5	20	45	80	125

b) On the axes opposite draw the graph of W against d^2.

c) Use the graph to find the relationship between W and d.

....

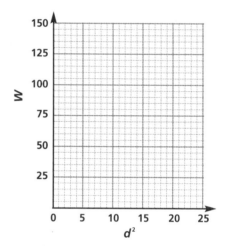

3 The time, t (hours), taken to travel a given distance is inversely proportional to the average speed, s (km/h).

a) Complete the table below.

$\frac{1}{s}$					
s	100	50	25	10	5
t	1	2	4	10	20

b) Plot the graph of t against $\frac{1}{s}$.

c) What is the relationship between t and s?

....

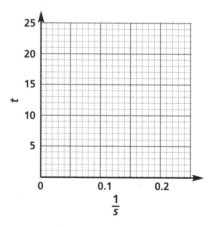

---

4 The tread, t (mm), of a lorry tyre is inversely proportional to the distance travelled, d (10 000 miles). Values for t and d are given in the table.

d (10 000 miles)	1	2	4	10
t (mm)	10	5	2.5	1

a) Draw a graph of t against $\frac{1}{d}$.

b) Use the relationship between t and d to calculate the tread on a tyre after 80 000 miles.

Angles

1 For each diagram work out the size of angle p and angle q, giving a reason for your answer.

They are not drawn to scale.

a)

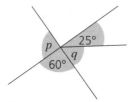

Angle p = ...

Reason: ....

....

Angle q = ...

Reason: ....

....

b)

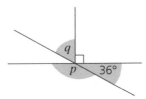

Angle p = ...

Reason: ....

....

Angle q = ...

Reason: ....

....

c)

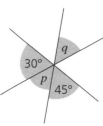

Angle p = ...

Reason: ....

....

Angle q = ...

Reason: ....

....

d)

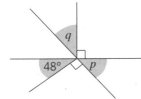

Angle p = ...

Reason: ....

....

Angle q = ...

Reason: ....

....

e)

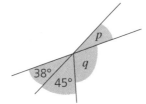

Angle p = ...

Reason: ....

....

Angle q = ...

Reason: ....

....

f)

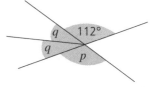

Angle p = ...

Reason: ....

....

Angle q = ...

Reason: ....

....

2 For each diagram work out the size of angle c and angle d giving a reason for your answer.

They are not drawn to scale.

a)

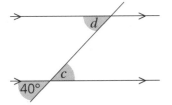

Angle c = ...

Reason: ....

....

Angle d = ...

Reason: ....

....

b)

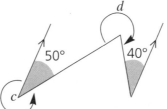

Angle c = ...

Reason: ....

....

Angle d = ...

Reason: ....

....

c)

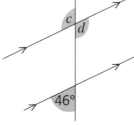

Angle c = ...

Reason: ....

....

Angle d = ...

Reason: ....

....

Angles

3. For each diagram work out the size of angle *m* and angle *n*, giving a reason for your answer. They are not drawn to scale.

a)
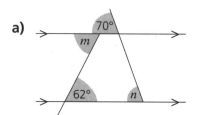

Angle *m* = ...

Reason: ....

....

Angle *n* = ...

Reason: ....

....

b)

Angle *m* = ...

Reason: ....

....

Angle *n* = ...

Reason: ....

....

c)
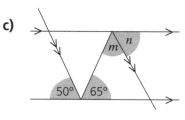

Angle *m* = ...

Reason: ....

....

Angle *n* = ...

Reason: ....

....

4. Work out the size of the angles marked *a*, *b* and *c*, giving reasons for your answer. The diagram is not drawn to scale.

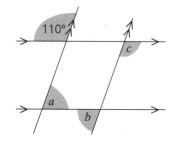

....

....

....

....

5. Work out the size of the angles marked *p*, *q*, *r* and *s*, giving reasons for your answer. The diagram is not drawn to scale.

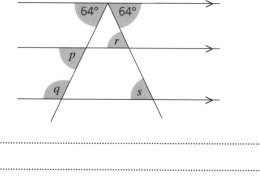

....

....

....

....

6. For each diagram work out the size of *x*. They are not drawn to scale.

a)
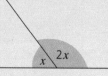

b)
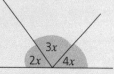

c)

d)
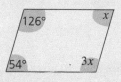

7. Draw a diagram and write a short explanation to prove that the interior angles of a triangle add up to 180°.

8. Draw a diagram and write a short explanation to prove that the exterior angle of a triangle is equal to the sum of the interior angles at the other two vertices.

LONSDALE

REVISION PLUS

Edexcel
GCSE Mathematics
for A*

Workbook Answers

Answers

Edexcel GCSE Maths for A*

Revision Plus

Page 4
1. a) i) 7.3 ii) 7.32 b) i) 16.8 ii) 16.78 c) i) 0.02 ii) 0.018
   d) i) 0.1 ii) 0.105 e) i) 7.1 ii) 7.07
2. **Lowest** 68.35kg, **Highest** 68.45kg
3. **Lowest** 1.645m, **Highest** 1.655m
4. a) i) 400 ii) 430 b) i) 9000 ii) 9200 c) i) 10 000 ii) 10 050
   d) i) 0.02 ii) 0.024 e) i) 0.00017 ii) 0.000174 f) i) 0.010 ii) 0.0104
5. 5749 − 5650 = 99
6. a) 135.7 b) 135.67 c) 100 d) 140 e) 136
7. a) 0.1 b) 0.06 c) 0.060 d) 0.06 e) 0.060 f) 0.0604
8. 47.65 − 47.55 = 0.1kg
9. a) 14.303 036 b) 14.3 (3 s.f.) or 14.30 (2 d.p.)

Page 5
1.

	100 Hundreds	10 Tens	1 Units	DECIMAL POINT	$\frac{1}{10}$ Tenths	$\frac{1}{100}$ Hundredths	$\frac{1}{1000}$ Thousandths	
a)	1	0	2	•	5			102.5
b)		1	3		4	7	1	13.471
c)			8		4	0	7	8.407
d)		9	0		0	3	1	90.031
e)	4	2	3		0	0	8	423.008

2. a) 0.6̇ b) 0.4 c) 0.0̈9̈ d) 0.7̇
3. 0.306, 0.36, 0.63, 3.6, 6.3
4. a) $\frac{7}{9}$ b) $\frac{7}{11}$ c) $\frac{5}{6}$ d) $2\frac{4}{11}$
5. a) 0.375 b) 0.2̇ c) 0.0̇3̇ d) 0.88 e) 0.26̇
6. a) 143.2, 14.32, 14.23, 13.42, 1.432, 1.342
   b) $3\frac{4}{5}$, 3.45, 3.405, $3\frac{2}{5}$, $3\frac{1}{20}$, 3.045
7. a) $\frac{1}{9}$ b) $\frac{5}{11}$ c) $1\frac{4}{9}$

Page 6
1. a) 47 b) 132.46 c) 0.146 d) 136 300 e) 98.28 f) 10.856
2. a) 97.2 b) 9.72 c) 0.972 d) 270 e) 3.6 f) 27
3. a) 1.63 b) 0.0347 c) 146.324 d) 0.0012467 e) 4.7 f) 34.2
4. a) 13 b) 0.13 c) 130 d) 728 e) 7.28 f) 728
5. £109.97
6. £47
7. 60 tickets
8. 14 days

Page 7
1. a) 4, 6, 20 b) 4, 20 c) 3, 15 d) 3, 6, 7, 21 e) 7, 21 f) 4, 6, 20
   g) 3, 7, 11 h) 4
2. a) 5, 11, 19, 31, 47, 81 b) 8, 24, 36 c) 5, 11, 22 d) 24, 36, 81
   e) 8, 24, 36 f) 5, 11, 19, 31, 47 g) 36, 81
3. a) $\frac{1}{8}$ or 0.125 b) 2 c) $\frac{4}{3}$ or $1\frac{1}{3}$ d) $\frac{3}{7}$
4. 10
5. a) $2^2 \times 3^2$ b) 2^6 c) $2 \times 3 \times 5 \times 31$

Page 8
6. a) 4 b) 180
7. a) 4 b) 1600
8. a) 3 b) 120
9. a) 12 and 20 **or** 4 and 60 b) **Accept any three of:** 15, 30, 45, 90
10. a) i) 25, 50, 100 ii) 25, 50, 100 iii) 14, 70, 84 iv) 29, 41, 61 b) 50
11. a) $\frac{1}{100}$, 0.01 b) 100 c) 100 d) $\frac{100}{99}$, $1\frac{1}{99}$, 1.0̇1̇
12. a) $2 \times 3 \times 5$ b) $2^2 \times 5^2$ c) 2^{11}
13. a) 3, 90 b) 2, 1160 c) 3, 360

Page 9
1. a) 8 b) 1 c) 64 d) 1000 e) 81 f) 1 g) 1 h) 6.25
2. a) 25, 64, 196 b) 27, 64, 125 c) 64 d) 64 e) 80
3. a) 9 b) -27 c) 25 d) -125 e) 1 f) -1 g) 81 h) 1 000 000

Page 10
4. a) 32 b) $\frac{1}{3}$ or 0.3̇ c) 4096 d) 2 e) 100 f) 1296 g) $\frac{1}{36}$ or 0.028 h) 4096
   i) 1 000 000 j) 1024 k) 1
5. a) T b) F (<) c) T d) F (=)
6. a) $n = 7$ b) $n = -3$ c) $n = \frac{1}{3}$
7. a) 8 b) 10 000 c) 16 d) 1
8. a) 256 b) 4 c) 1024 d) 1600 e) $1\frac{1}{27}$ or 1.037̇ f) 27 g) 2 h) 5 i) 2
9. a) 3^7 b) 2^4 c) 4^5

Page 11
1. a) 5 b) 6 c) $\frac{1}{6}$ d) 14 e) 4 f) 1 g) $\frac{1}{2}$ h) -10 i) $\frac{1}{9}$
2. a) 4, 36, 64 b) 8, 27, 64 c) 64 d) 10 e) 36
3. a) 4 b) $\frac{1}{25}$ c) 20 d) 30 e) 32 f) 64
4. a) 4^2 b) 3^2 c) 2^4 d) 6^2

5. a) $x = 2$ b) $x = 3$
6. a) $3\sqrt{6}$ b) $3\sqrt{10}$ c) $\sqrt{5}$ d) $32 - 10\sqrt{7}$
7. a) $\frac{4\sqrt{7}}{7}$ b) $\frac{5\sqrt{11}}{11}$
8. a) 13 b) 5 c) 9 d) 5 e) 15
9. a) 27 b) 4 c) 4 d) $\frac{1}{4}$ e) 16
10. a) $10\sqrt{2}$ b) $4\sqrt{5}$ c) $3\sqrt{7}$ d) 25 − 7 = 18 e) $(2 - \sqrt{3})$

Page 12
1. a) 17 b) 7 c) 44 d) 11 e) 11 f) 1 g) 200 h) 4 i) -16
2. a) $(13 - 3) \times 4 + 3$ b) $13 - 3 \times (4 + 3)$ c) $(13 - 3) \times (4 + 3)$
   d) $13 - (3 \times 4) + 3$ e) $(3 \times 1.4 + 4) \times 2.5$ f) $7 + 3.2 \times (6 - 4.4)$
3. a) 43 b) -1 c) -35 d) 11 e) 12 f) 10 g) -1.5 h) 54 i) -25
4. a) $3^2 - (4 \times 5) + 10$ b) $(3^2 - 4) \times 5 + 10$ c) $3^2 - (4 \times (5 + 10))$
5. a) $(4^2 - 3) \times 4 + 2$ b) $4^2 - 3 \times (4 + 2)$ c) $4^2 - (3 \times 4) + 2$

Page 13
1. a) 230 b) 2300 c) 42 100 d) 63.2 e) 7467 f) 0.03 g) 0.0023
   h) 0.000 421 i) 0.063 24
2. a) 6×10^2 b) 4.73×10^2 c) 4.2×10^4 d) 4.13256×10^5 e) 4.963×10^2
   f) 3.2×10^2 g) 4.7×10^1 h) 6.31×10^{-4} i) 1×10^{-1}
3. a) 1.55×10^8 b) 14 c) 2.17×10^8
4. a) 5.633×10^3 b) 6.182×10^5 c) 8.424×10^{11} d) 5×10^{-2}
5. 7.49×10^6, 9.34×10^6, 8.14×10^7, 2.43×10^8
6. a) 1.08×10^{12} metres b) 9.4608×10^{15} metres c) 8 mins
   d) 4.068144×10^{16} metres (assuming 365 days in 1 year)

Page 14
1. a) $\frac{16}{40}$, $\frac{40}{100}$, $\frac{10}{25}$ b) $\frac{35}{50}$, $\frac{28}{40}$, $\frac{84}{120}$
2. a) $\frac{9}{10}$ b) 7 c) $\frac{4}{5}$ d) $\frac{27}{46}$
3. a) $\frac{1}{2}$, $\frac{3}{5}$, $\frac{2}{3}$, $\frac{11}{15}$, $\frac{5}{6}$ b) $\frac{9}{10}$, $\frac{5}{8}$, $\frac{3}{5}$, $\frac{1}{4}$, $\frac{9}{40}$
4. **Accept any correct answer, e.g.: a)** $\frac{17}{20}$ **b)** $\frac{13}{30}$
5. $\frac{22}{30}$, $\frac{23}{30}$, $\frac{24}{30}$ **(any two or equivalent)**
6. a) i) $2\frac{1}{5}$ ii) $2\frac{1}{6}$ iii) $4\frac{4}{5}$ iv) $10\frac{2}{3}$ b) i) $\frac{10}{3}$ ii) $\frac{21}{4}$ iii) $\frac{58}{5}$ iv) $\frac{401}{20}$
7. a) **Accept any three suitable answers, e.g.:** $\frac{4}{6}$, $\frac{6}{9}$, $\frac{8}{12}$, $\frac{10}{15}$, etc.
   b) **Accept any three suitable answers, e.g.:** $\frac{4}{7}$, $\frac{8}{14}$, $\frac{12}{21}$, $\frac{16}{28}$, etc.
   c) **Accept any three suitable answers, e.g.:** $\frac{9}{11}$, $\frac{18}{22}$, $\frac{27}{33}$, $\frac{36}{44}$, etc.
8. $\frac{1}{2}$, $\frac{3}{4}$, $\frac{4}{5}$, $\frac{9}{10}$, $\frac{19}{20}$
9. **Accept any three from:** $\frac{17}{20}$, $\frac{33}{40}$, $\frac{34}{40}$, $\frac{35}{40}$, $\frac{41}{50}$, $\frac{42}{50}$, $\frac{43}{50}$, $\frac{44}{50}$

Page 15
1. a) $1\frac{5}{12}$ b) $1\frac{7}{12}$ c) $7\frac{2}{5}$ d) $11\frac{23}{24}$ e) $\frac{2}{5}$ f) $\frac{1}{5}$ g) $3\frac{17}{40}$ h) $4\frac{17}{30}$
2. $\frac{1}{3}$
3. a) $\frac{1}{10}$ b) $\frac{9}{35}$ c) $\frac{5}{6}$ d) $1\frac{1}{2}$ e) $5\frac{3}{5}$ f) $5\frac{4}{7}$ g) $1\frac{11}{16}$ h) $\frac{2}{3}$ i) $3\frac{5}{9}$ j) $\frac{7}{30}$
4. a) $1\frac{13}{40}$ b) $6\frac{17}{24}$ c) $\frac{7}{30}$ d) $\frac{4}{5}$ e) $\frac{7}{25}$ f) $1\frac{1}{12}$ g) $5\frac{5}{12}$ h) $1\frac{1}{5}$ i) $22\frac{1}{2}$ j) $\frac{7}{18}$

Page 16
1. £30
2. a) £5200 b) £162.50 c) $\frac{11}{20}$
3. a) £78.00 b) £145.80
4. $\frac{5}{6}$
5. a) i) £300 ii) £225 b) £400
6. $\frac{1}{90}$

Page 17
1. a) 4%, $\frac{6}{16}$, 0.38 b) $\frac{2}{3}$, 70%, $\frac{11}{15}$, 0.75
2. a) 12p b) 1.95km
3. a) 20% b) 5%
4. a) i) 0.54m ii) 45% b) i) 24kg ii) 60%
5. 12.5%
6. a) £1.17 b) 5.12kg c) £0.52
7. a) 66.6̇% b) 0.1% c) 27.5%
8. 30%
9. 17.5%

Page 18
1. £11 550
2. 34 450
3. a) £145 200 b) 1.21
4. a) £5120 b) 0.512
5. No, 10% off sale price so the fridge will cost £72
6. a) 113.4kg b) 0.945

Page 19
1. 40 mins
2. £144

3. £4500

4. 220km

5. £60 000

6. a) £95 400 **b)** £107 191 **c)** £161 176

7. a) £10837.50 **b)** £9211.88 **c)** £6655.58

8. £124

9. £3200

10. 300 stamps

11. Simple £23600, Compound £23484.83. Simple earns more.

Page 20

1. a) 2 : 1 **b)** 1 : 0.5

2. a) 2 : 3 **b)** 1 : 1.5

3. a) 3 : 4 **b)** 1 : 1.$\dot{3}$

4. a) 9 : 5 **b)** 18 : 11 **c)** Large tin offers best value at 0.08p per g, compared to small tin at 0.088p per g

5. a) 32p : 48p **b)** 1m 40cm : 2m 10cm : 2m 80cm

6. Susan is 60, Janet is 36 and Polly is 24 years old

7. £4750 and £5250

Page 21

1. 7 : 5

2. 2778kg

3. a) 225g flour, 325g oatmeal and 200g margarine. **b)** 55 biscuits

4. a) 8 : 3 **b)** 1 : 0.375

5. The small tub represents the best value at 19p per 100g, compared to the large tub at 22p per 100g

6. £65

7. 160°

8. £1.68

9. a) 1.75km **b)** 5.4cm

Page 22

1. a) 36 **b)** 20

2. a) 1 **b)** $\sqrt{3}$

3. 1.5cm

4. 20N/cm^2

5. a) 300 **b)** 11

6. a) 2.5 **b)** 0.08

Page 23

1. a) Upper 7.45cm, **Lower** 7.35cm **b) Greatest** 4.3cm, **Shortest** 4.1cm

2. 5.3%

3. a) 24.65cm **b)** 24.55cm **c)** 18.75cm to 18.85cm

4. a) 19.0575m^2 **b)** 18.1875m^2 **c)** 18.1875m$^2 \leq$ Area < 19.0575m^2 **d) Upper** 17.6m, **Lower** 17.2m

5. a) 523.018cm^2 **b)** 428.035cm^2

6. 1.412 hrs to 1.418 hrs

Page 24

1. a) i) $100 \times 50 = 5000$ **ii)** 5618 **b) i)** $4 \times 15 = 60$ **ii)** 57.76 **c) i)** $\frac{30 \times 6}{20} = 9$ **ii)** 8.7 **d) i)** $400\,000 \times 0.0007 = 280$ **ii)** 273.155 46

2. a) i) $7 + 9 + 13 = £29$ **ii)** £29.73 John's calculation is accurate **b) i)** $9 + 17 + 5 = £31$ **ii)** £30.20 Donna's calculation is inaccurate

3. a) $10 + 30 + 40 = 80$, inaccurate 85 **b)** $9 + 10 + 7 + 14 = 40$, accurate **c)** $(3 \times 6) + 90 - 10 = 98$, inaccurate 100.75 **d)** $(5 \times 6) + (1 \times 10) = 40$, inaccurate 37.21

Page 25

1. a) $11p$ **b)** a^2 **c)** $11w^2$ **d)** $6a + 8b$ **e)** $-2c + 2d$ **f)** $-2ab + 9cd$ **g)** $-x^2 - 5x + 9$ **h)** $17 - 6p^2 + 7p$ **i)** $6ab$ **j)** $24pqr$ **k)** $12s^2t^3$ **l)** $\frac{9b^2c}{a}$

2. x can take any value and the identity will hold true because both sides are equal to $5x$.

3. a) a^5 **b)** $12b^4$ **c)** $24p^5q^2$ **d)** r^4 **e)** $4c$ **f)** $2ab$ **g)** $5a^2b$ **h)** $8a^6b^3$ **i)** $20p^3q^6$

4. a) $2ab$ **b)** $16a^2$ **c)** $8a$ **d)** $9b^2c$

5. a) $n^{\frac{3}{2}}$ **b)** a^{10} **c)** $\pm 6n^2$

6. a) $18x$ **b)** $6x$ **c)** $72x^2$ **d)** 2 **e)** $-7p^2$ **f)** $21ab + 3bc$ **g)** $9ab + 7a^2b + 8ab^2$

7. a) a^9 **b)** $30x^8$ **c)** x^2 **d)** $2abc$ **e)** $64a^6$ **f)** $81a^8b^4$

8. $x^2 + 7x + 9 = (x + 3)^2$. $x = 11$

Page 26

1. a) 19 **b)** 14 **c)** 20 **d)** 20 **e)** -15 **f)** -40 **g)** 24 **h)** -2 **i)** 98 **j)** $-\frac{2}{5}$

2. a) $\frac{5}{6}$ **b)** -1 **c)** 2 **d)** 0

3. a) -16 **b)** 32 **c)** 64 **d)** 24 **e)** 60

4. a) 24 **b)** -32 **c)** -1 **d)** 7 **e)** $4\frac{1}{4}$ **f)** 1 **g)** 4 **h)** -2 **i)** 23 **j)** 1 **k)** $\frac{7}{12}$ **l)** 33

5. a) 77 **b)** -35 **c)** 17 **d)** 15 **e)** -24

6. a) 1.5×10^8 **b)** 3.5×10^4 **c)** 4.3×10^3

Page 27

1. a) $8x + 4$ **b)** $9r - 21$ **c)** $6m^2 + 4m$ **d)** $8p - 2p^2$ **e)** $6r^3 - 18r$

f) $40x^3 - 30x^2$ **g)** $10y + 23$ **h)** $17x - 15x^2$ **i)** $46x - 33x^3$ **j)** $19x - 2$ **k)** $42x - 1$ **l)** $10x^2 - 27x + 4$ **m)** $x^2 + 7x + 10$ **n)** $2x^2 + 11x + 12$ **o)** $6x^2 - x - 2$ **p)** $4x^2 - 21x + 5$ **q)** $x^2 - 9$ **r)** $16x^2 - 8x + 1$

2. a) $5(x + 2)$ **b)** $4(x - 2)$ **c)** $2(3x + 5y)$ **d)** $3x(2 + x)$ **e)** $5x(2x - 1)$ **f)** $2xy(3x - 5)$ **g)** $2pqr(2pq^2 + 3)$ **h)** $(3y + 2)(x + z)$ **i)** $(4y + 3)(x + 4y + 3)$

3. a) $24x - 6y$ **b)** $6x^2 + 15x$ **c)** $8x^2y - 4x^3$ **d)** $18x - 6x^3$ **e)** $13x - 23$ **f)** $12x^2 - 14x + 20$ **g)** $40x^3 + 18x^2 + 6x$ **h)** $12x^2 + 14x + 4$ **i)** $25x^2 - 36$ **j)** $8x^3 + 14x^2 + 6x$ **k)** $8x^3 - 6x^5 - 12 + 9x^2$

4. a) $3(3x - 5)$ **b)** $9(x + 1)$ **c)** $x(20x - 1)$ **d)** $4x(1 - 5x^2)$ **e)** $4xy(5xy + 9)$ **f)** $(3x - 5)(4 + y)$

5. a) $a^2 + 2ab + b^2$ **b)** 100

Page 28

1. a) $x = 7$ **b)** $x = 4$ **c)** $x = 3$ **d)** $x = 4$ **e)** $x = 5$ **f)** $x = -\frac{1}{2}$ **g)** $x = 18$ **h)** $x = 15$ **i)** $x = 13$ **j)** $x = 3$ **k)** $x = 1.5$ **l)** $x = -8$ **m)** $x = \frac{1}{2}$ **n)** $x = 4.5$ **o)** $x = 3$ **p)** $x = 1.5$ **q)** $x = -4$ **r)** $x = -2$ **s)** $x = 4$ **t)** $x = 6$ **u)** $x = 7$

Page 29

2. a) $x + 2x + 2x + 4 = 5x + 4$ **b)** $5x + 4 = 64$; $x = 12$; Helen is 28 years old

3. a) $4x + 2$cm **b)** $4x + 2 = 50$; $x = 12$cm

4. a) $6(x + 5)$ **or** $6x + 30$ **b)** $6(x + 5) = 72$; $x = 7$cm

5. a) $x = 6$ **b)** $x = -4$ **c)** $x = 6$ **d)** $x = -5$ **e)** $x = -7.5$ **f)** $x = -4$ **g)** $x = 6$ **h)** $x = 3$ **i)** $x = 2$ **j)** $x = 4$ **k)** $x = 2.5$ **l)** $x = 3.5$ **m)** $x = 1.4$ **n)** $x = 3$ **o)** $x = -1$ **p)** $x = 2$ **q)** $x = 3$ **r)** $x = 1.5$

6. a) $3x = 180°$; $x = 60°$ **b)** $17x + 20° = 360°$; $x = 20°$ **c)** $\frac{20}{3}x + 20° = 180°$; $x = 24°$

Page 30

1. a) $x = 3 - 4y$ **b)** $x = \frac{50 - 7y}{6}$ **c)** $x = \frac{3y + 5}{7}$ **d)** $x = y(z - 5)$ **or** $x = yz - 5y$ **e)** $x = 20 - 3y$ **f)** $x = \frac{8y + 3}{4}$ **g)** $x = \frac{18 - 3y}{8}$ **h)** $x = \pm\frac{\sqrt{3y}}{2}$ **i)** $x = \pm\sqrt{(6)y}$ **j)** $x = \pm\sqrt{\frac{7y - 3}{5}}$ **k)** $x = \frac{b}{c(d^2 + 1)}$ **l)** $x = \sqrt{\frac{m}{t^2 - 1}}$

2. $V = 160$cm^3

Page 31

3. $s = 44$m

4. 100°C

5. a) $A = \pi\left(\frac{C}{2\pi}\right)^2 = \pi \times \frac{C^2}{4\pi^2} = \frac{C^2}{4\pi}$ **b)** $A = 130$cm^3

6. a) $p = \frac{4q + 3}{4}$ **b)** $p = \frac{4 - q}{6}$ **c)** $p = \frac{11q - 15}{2}$ **d)** $p = \sqrt{\frac{8q - 4}{3}}$ **e)** $p = \sqrt{\frac{8q + 6}{3}}$

7. $A = 1.08$m^2

8. $r = 5.6$cm

9. a) $l = \frac{T^2g}{4\pi^2}$ **b)** $l = 0.248$

Page 32

1. a) $(x + 4)(x + 2)$ **b)** $(x + 5)(x + 2)$ **c)** $(x + 10)(x - 1)$ **d)** $(x + 10)(x - 2)$ **e)** $(x - 10)(x + 10)$ **f)** $(x - 12)(x + 12)$

2. a) $(2x - 1)(x + 3)$ **b)** $(4x - 1)(x + 1)$ **c)** $(2x + 1)(x + 3)$ **d)** $(3x + 2)(2x - 1)$ **e)** $(2y - 5)(3y + 2)$ **f)** $(4n - 1)(3n - 2)$

3. $(x + 3)(-2x + 1)$

4. a) $(x + 3)(x + 2)$ **b)** $(x - 3)(x - 2)$ **c)** $(x + 6)(x - 1)$ **d)** $(x - 6)(x + 1)$ **e)** $(x + 6)(x - 5)$ **f)** $(x + 30)(x + 1)$ **g)** $(x - 9)(x + 9)$ **h)** $(x - 13)(x + 13)$

5. a) $2(n - 7)(2n - 3)$ **b)** $(5y - 2)^2$ **c)** $(2x - 3)(-3x + 1)$

6. a) $(n + 7)(7n + 3)$ **b)** $107 \times 703 = 75\,221$ – the coefficients of $7n^2 + 52n + 21$ match the digits in 75 221. If $n = 100$, $7n^2 = 70\,000$ and $52n = 5200$, so $7n^2 + 52n + 21 = 75\,221$. By substituting this value for n into the factorised equation we get $(100 + 7)(7 \times 100 + 3) = 107 \times 703$ **c)** $3n^2 + 22n + 7$

Page 33

1. a) $(a + 3)(a - 2) = 0$; $a = -3$ or $a = 2$ **b)** $(a + 5)(a - 1) = 0$; $a = -5$ or $a = 1$ **c)** $(a - 4)(a + 2) = 0$; $a = 4$ or $a = -2$ **d)** $(a - 3)(2a + 1) = 0$; $a = 3$ or $a = -\frac{1}{2}$ **e)** $(a + 4)(3a + 2) = 0$; $a = -4$ or $a = \frac{-2}{3}$ **f)** $(2a + 3)(4a - 3) = 0$; $a = -1\frac{1}{2}$ or $a = \frac{3}{4}$

2. a) $x = -6$ or $x = 1$ **b)** $x = 7$ or $x = 4$ **c)** $x = 2$ or $x = 1$

3. a) $x^2 + 2x = 80$ **b)** $x = 8$ **c)** 36cm

4. a) $n + 1$ **b)** $2n^2 + 2n + 1$ **c)** 5 and -6

Page 34

1. a) $x = 0.39$ or $x = -10.39$ **b)** $x = 9.90$ or $x = 0.12$ **c)** $x = 4.65$ or $x = -0.65$

2. a) $x^2 + 22x + 120$ **b)** $x^2 + 22x$ **c)** $x = 4$m

3. a) $x = 6.54$ or $x = 0.46$ **b)** $a = 4$ or $a = \frac{3}{4}$ **c)** $x = 5$ or $x = -4$

d) $x = 0.4$ or $x = -12.4$ **e)** $a = 5$ or $a = -7$ **f)** $y = \frac{1}{2}$ or $y = 1\frac{1}{2}$
4. $n^2 - n = 72$; $n = 9$ or $n = -8$
5. 10

Page 35
1. a) $x = -1.78$ or $x = 0.28$ **b)** $x = 0.56$ or $x = -3.56$
c) $x = 0.35$ or $x = -1.15$
2. a) $2x^2 - 4x + 4 = 144$ **b)** $2x^2 - 4x - 140 = 0$; $x^2 - 2x - 70 = 0$ **c)** $x = 9.43$
3. a) $x = 1.4$ or $x = -3.4$ **b)** $x = 1$ or $x = 3$ **c)** $x = 2.8$ or $x = -1.8$
d) $x = 0.4$ or $x = -10.4$ **e)** $x = 1.5$ or $x = -0.5$ **f)** $x = 0.7$ or $x = -5.7$
4. a) $4w^2 + 80w$ or $4(w^2 + 20w)$ **b)** $4w^2 + 80w - 400 = 0$ **c)** Divide all terms by 4: $w^2 + 20w - 100 = 0$ **d)** 4.1cm

Page 36
1. $x = 2.6$
2. $x = 3.23$
3. a) $x^2(x + 3) = x^3 + 3x^2$ **b)** $x = 2.7$cm
4. a) $x = 1.8$ **b)** $x = 4.52$
5. a) $(2x)(x)(x + 3) = 2x^3 + 6x^2$ **b)** $x = 2.2$cm

Page 37
1. i) 31, 63 **ii)** -17, -33 **b) i)** 18, 34 **ii)** -14, -30
2. 25, 36, 49, 64 **b)** 15, 21, 28, 36
3. a) 23 **b)** 58
4. a) -3 **b)** 21
5. a) 14th **b)** 2nd
6. a) 9th **b)** 12th
7. a) 29 **b)** -16 **c)** 13th **d)** 19th

Page 38
7. $2n + 1$; 11, 13, 15, 17, 19
8. $-2n + 8$; -2, -4, -6, -8, -10
9. a) $s = 4n - 3$ **b)** 29 **c)** 13th diagram
10. a) $c = 3n$ **b)** 45 **c)** 27th diagram
11. See p.8 for diagrams
12. a) 11 **b)** 22nd
13. a) $-4n + 19$ **b) i)** -21 **ii)** -381

Page 39
1. See p.8 for graph
2. a) $y = \frac{1}{2}x + 4$ **b) See p.8 for graph c)** $p = 6.5$ **d)** $q = -8$
3. a) $y = 3x - 4$ **b) See p.8 for graph c)** $y = 0.5$ **d)** $x = 2.4$
4. a) See p.8 for graph b) $x = 2.5$ **c)** $x = 2.5$

Page 40
1. a) gradient 2, intercept (0,1) **b)** gradient -3, intercept (0, 5)
c) gradient -1, intercept (0,3) **d)** gradient -2, intercept (0,1.75)
e) gradient 1, intercept (0,4.5) **f)** gradient 2, intercept (0,2)
2. Line 1: $y = -x + 3$, Line 2: $y = 5 - 3x$, Line 3: $y = 2x + 1$
Line 4: $y = 2x + 2$
3. a) $y = 2x + 1$ **b)** $y = -2x + 1$ **c)** $y = 2x - 2$ **d)** $y = x - 2$ **e)** $y = x + 3$
f) $y = x - 3.5$
4. a) gradient -3, intercept (0,-3) **b)** gradient $\frac{3}{4}$, intercept (0,2)
c) gradient $\frac{1}{2}$, intercept (0,1.5) **d)** gradient $\frac{1}{2}$, intercept (0,-1.5)
e) gradient $\frac{1}{2}$, intercept (0,1.5) **f)** gradient 2, intercept (0,15)
g) gradient 4, intercept (0,5)
5. a) $y = x + 4$ **b)** $y = -x$
6. i), iii) **and** iv)
7. ii) **and** iii)

Page 41
1. a) $x > 9$ **b)** $x < 17$ **c)** $x \leq 5$ **d)** $x \leq 2$ **e)** $x \leq 3$ **f)** $x < 3$

9 10 11   15 16 17   3 4 5   0 1 2   1 2 3   1 2 3
2. a) $x < -2$ **b)** $x > -3$ **c)** $x \geq -1$ **d)** $x \geq 1.5$ **e)** $x \geq 2.5$ **f)** $x \geq -2.5$
3. a)–d) See p.8 for graphs

Page 42
4. a) See p.8 for graph b) (2,3)
5. a) See p.8 for graph b) (3,2)
6. See p.8 for graph
7. $y < 4$, $x \geq -1$, $y \geq x$, $y \geq -x + 2$
8. a) $x \geq 5$ **b)** $x > 2$ **c)** $x \leq 5.5$ **d)** $x < -2$

5 6 7 8   2 3 4   3 4 5 6   -5 -4 -3 -2
e) $x < 4$ **f)** $x \geq -2$ **g)** $x < -14$

1 2 3 4   -2 -1 0 1   -17 -16 -15 -14
9. See p.9 for graph

10. See p.9 for graph

Page 43
1. a) $x = 3$, $y = 2$ **b)** $x = 7$, $y = 2$ **c)** $x = 5$, $y = -2$ **d)** $x = 6$, $y = 1$
e) $x = 4$, $y = 3$ **f)** $x = 3$, $y = 1$
2. $2d + c = 84$, $3d + 2c = 138$; $c = 24p$, $d = 30p$
3. a) $x = 2$, $y = 4$ **b)** $x = 3$, $y = 6$, **c)** $x = 4$, $y = -2$ **d)** $x = -3$, $y = 4$
e) $x = 1.5$, $y = 3.5$ **f)** $x = -3$, $y = -0.5$ **g)** $x = -3$, $y = -2$ **h)** $x = 1.5$, $y = -7.5$

Page 44
1. a) See p.9 for graph b) $x = 3$, $y = 11$
2. a) See p.9 for graph b) $x = 3$, $y = 19$
3. a) See p.9 for graph b) i) $x = -0.8$, $y = 1.2$ **ii)** $x = 1$, $y = 3$
iii) $x = 4$, $y = 0$
4. a) See p.9 for graph b) $x = 2$, $y = 9$
5. a) See p.9 for graph b) i) $x = 2$, $y = 4$ **ii)** $x = 5$, $y = 1$
iii) $x = -1$, $y = -5$

Page 45
1. a) $x = \frac{1}{5}$, $y = \frac{1}{5}$ and $x = -3$, $y = 45$
b) $x = 1.6$, $y = 25.6$ and $x = -1.5$, $y = 22.5$
2. a) $x = 0$, $y = 1$ and $x = 1$, $y = 0$
b) $x = 2.87$, $y = -0.87$ and $x = -0.87$, $y = 2.87$

Page 46
1. a) See p.9 for graph $x = -0.6$, $y = 0.4$ and $x = 1.6$, $y = 2.6$
b) $0.4 - -0.6 = 1$✔, $2.6 - 1.6 = 1$✔
2. a) See p.9 for graph $x = 0.9$, $y = 2.9$ and $x = -2.9$, $y = -0.9$
b) $x = -0.9$, $y = 2.9$ and $x = 2.9$, $y = -0.9$
3. a) i) $x = 1.3$, $y = 3.4$ and $x = -0.8$, $y = 1.2$ **ii)** $x = 0.7$, $y = 0.3$ and
$x = -2.7$, $y = 3.7$ **iii)** $x = 0.6$, $y = 0.4$ and $x = -1.6$, $y = 2.6$
b) See p.9 for graphs i) $x = 1.3$, $y = 3.4$ and $x = -0.8$, $y = 1.2$
ii) $x = 0.7$, $y = 0.3$ and $x = -2.7$, $y = 3.7$ **iii)** $x = 0.6$, $y = 0.4$
and $x = -1.6$, $y = 2.6$
4. a) See p.9 for graph $x = 0.9$, $y = 1.8$ and $x = -0.9$, $y = -1.8$
b) See p.9 for graph $x = -0.85$, $y = 2.85$ and $x = 2.85$, $y = 0.85$
c) See p.9 for graph $x = -0.9$, $y = 0.4$ and $x = 0.9$, $y = 0.4$

Page 47
**For pages 47–49, where answers are taken from a graph, accept
values up to 0.1 either side of the answers given below.**
1. a) See p.10 for graph b) i) $y = 0.25$ **ii)** $x = \pm 1.8/1.9$
2. a)

x^2	-3	-2	-1	0	1	2
$2x^2$	18	8	2	0	2	8
$+ x$	-3	-2	-1	0	1	2
$- 5$	$- 5$	$- 5$	$- 5$	$- 5$	$- 5$	$- 5$
$y = 2x^2 + x - 5$	10	1	-4	-5	-2	5

b) See p.10 for graph
c) i) $y = 5$ **ii)** $x = 1.6$ or -2.1
d) 1.5 or -1.8 **e)** 1.6 or -2 (exact) **f)** 1 exact or -1.4

Page 48
3. a)

x	-4	-3	-2	-1	0	1	2
x^2	16	9	4	1	0	1	4
$+ 2x$	-8	-6	-4	-2	0	+2	+4
$- 4$	$- 4$	$- 4$	$- 4$	$- 4$	$- 4$	$- 4$	$- 4$
$y = x^2 + 2x - 4$	4	-1	-4	-5	-4	-1	4

b) See p.10 for graph
c) i) $x = 1.2$, $x = -3.2$
ii) $x^2 + 2x - 4 = 2$, $x = 1.6$, $x = -3.6$
iii) $x^2 + 2x - 4 = -3$, $x = 0.4$, $x = -2.4$
4. a)

x	-4	-3	-2	-1	0	1	2	3	4
y	-6	1	6	9	10	9	6	1	-6

b) See p.10 for graph
c) i) $\pm\sqrt{10}$ **ii)** ± 2 **iii)** $\pm\sqrt{12}$
5. a) See p.10 for graph b) i) $x = \pm 3.5$ **ii)** $x = \pm 3.9$ **iii)** $x = \pm 2.4$

Page 49
1. a)

x	-3	-2	-1	0	1	2
x^3	-27	-8	-1	0	1	8
$+ 10$	+ 10	+ 10	+ 10	+ 10	+ 10	+ 10
$y = x^3 + 10$	-17	2	9	10	11	18

b) See p.10 for graph c) i) $x = -2.7$ **ii)** $y = 13.4$ **(Accept 12–14)**

2. a) See p.10 for graph **b) i)** 0.4 **ii)** -0.7

3. a)

x	-3	-2	-1	0	1	2	3
x^3	-27	-8	-1	0	1	8	27
-2	-2	-2	-2	-2	-2	-2	-2
$y = x^3 - 2$	-29	-10	-3	-2	-1	6	25

b) See p.10 for graph **c)** $x = 1.25$ **d) i)** $x = 2.8$ **ii)** $y = 1.4$

Page 50

1. a)

x	-2	-1	0	1	2
4^x	$\frac{1}{16}$	$\frac{1}{4}$	1	4	16

x	-2	-1	0	1	2
$\left(\frac{1}{4}\right)^x$	16	4	1	$\frac{1}{4}$	$\frac{1}{16}$

b) See p.10 for graph **c)** They are symmetrical, mirror line = y-axis

2. a) See p.10 for graph **b)** $a = 10$, $b = 2$, $y = 10 \times 2^x$

3. a)–c) See p.10 for graphs

4. a) $a = 2$, $b = 3$, $y = 2 \times 3^x$ **b)** See p.10 for graph

Page 51

1. a)

$x^{(o)}$	0	30	60	90	120	150	180	210	240	270	300	330	360
$y = \sin x$	0	0.5	0.866	1	0.866	0.5	0	-0.5	-0.866	-1	-0.866	-0.5	0

b) See p.10 for graph **c)** 53°, 127° (actual values) **d)** 0.7

2. a)

$x^{(o)}$	0	30	60	90	120	150	180	210	240	270	300	330	360
$y = \cos x$	1	0.866	0.5	0	-0.5	-0.866	-1	-0.866	-0.5	0	0.5	0.866	1

b) See p.10 for graph **c)** 53°, 307° (actual values) **d)** 0.7

3. a) See p.11 for graph **b)** It is not wave-like, it repeats every time.

Page 52

1. a)–b) See p.11 for graph
c) i) Translated down $\binom{0}{-4}$ **ii)** One way stretch in the y direction by factor 3

2. a) See p.11 for graph
b) i) One way stretch in y towards x-axis by factor $\frac{1}{2}$
ii) One way stretch in x towards y-axis by factor $\frac{1}{2}$

3. a) See p.11 for graph
b) i) Translated $\binom{-90}{0}$ left **ii)** Translated $\binom{0}{-1}$ down

4. See p.11 for graphs

5. See p.11 for graphs

6. See p.11 for graphs.

Page 53

1. a) 1.30pm **b)** Mr Brown **c)** Mr Smith 60mph
d) They passed each other **e)** Mr Smith, 30 mins

2. a) B **b)** A **c)** D **d)** C

3. a)

Pounds (£)	10	20	30	40
US Dollars ($)	14	28	42	56

b) See p.11 for graph **c)** Accept £21–22

4. a) See p.11 for graph **b)** Plumber A **c)** Plumber B **d)** After 4 hours

5. See p.11 for graph

Page 54

1. a) See p.11 for graph **b)** $N = 10t$

2. a)

d^2	0	1	4	9	16	25
d	0	1	2	3	4	5
W	0	5	20	45	80	125

b) See p.11 for graph **c)** $W = 5d^2$

3. a)

$\left(\frac{1}{s}\right)$	0.01	0.02	0.04	0.1	0.2
s	100	50	25	10	5
t	1	2	4	10	20

b) See p.12 for graph **c)** $t = \frac{100}{s}$

4. a) See p.12 for graph **b)** $t = \frac{10}{d}$, 1.25mm

Page 55

1. a) $p = 120°$ (angles on a straight line), $q = 95°$ (angles on a straight line)
b) $p = 144°$ (angles on a straight line), $q = 54°$ (angles on a straight line)
c) $p = 105°$ (angles on a straight line), $q = 105°$ (vertically opposite angles)
d) $p = 42°$ (angles on a straight line), $q = 48°$ (angles on a straight line)
e) $p = 38°$ (vertically opposite angles), $q = 97°$ (angles on a straight line)
f) $p = 112°$ (vertically opposite angles), $q = 34°$ (angles on a straight line)

2. a) $c = 40°$ (vertically opposite angles), $d = 40°$ (alternate angles)
b) $c = 310°$ (angles round a point, 360°−50°)
$d = 90°$ (draw a central line parallel to the other parallel lines, and use alternate angles, 50° + 40°)
c) $c = 134°$ (corresponding angles / angles on a straight line)
$d = 134°$ (vertically opposite angles)

Page 56

3. a) $m = 62°$ (alternate angles), $n = 70°$ (corresponding angles)
b) $m = 180° − 95° = 85°$ (allied / interior), $n = 70°$ (corresponding angles)
c) $m = 65°$ (alternate angles / angles on a straight line),
$n = 50°$ (n is corresponding to the angle alternate to the 50° angle)

4. $a = 70°$ (alternate angles / angles on a straight line), $b = 70°$ (alternate angles), $c = 110°$ (vertically opposite angles / co-interior / allied angles)

5. $p = 64°$ (corresponding angles), $q = 180° − 64° = 116°$ (alternate angles)
$r = 64°$ (alternate angles), $s = 64°$ (corresponding angles)

6. a) 60° **b)** 20° **c)** 36° **d)** 45°

7. Accept any suitable drawing (see p.12 for diagram) and explanation, e.g. $a = e$ corresponding, $b = d$ alternate, $c + d + e = 180°$, $a + b + c = 180°$

8. Accept any suitable drawing and explanation as for question 7 above.

Page 57

1. a) 60° **b)** 115°

2. a) 360° **b)** 360°

3. a) 4 sides **b)** 360°

4. a) 6 sides **b)** 360°

5. 74°

6. a) 5 sides **b)** $x = 80$ **c)** 100°, 80°, 20°, 30°, 130°

7. a) 108° **b)** 72° **c)** 5

8. 36 sides

Page 58

1. a) $x = 70°$ parallelogram (Opposite sides are parallel) **b)** $x = 50°$ kite (One line of symmetry and two pairs of adjacent equal sides.)
c) $x = 75°$ trapezium (Just one pair of parallel sides) **d)** $x = 110°$ rhombus (All sides equal but angles not right angles)

2. a) Rhombus **b)** Rectangle **c)** Square

3. $a + b + c = 180°$, $d + e + f = 180°$, $a + b + c + d + e + f = 360°$
See p.12 for diagram

4. a) $p = 56°$ **b)** $p = 107°$, $q = 95°$ **c)** $p = 60°$ **d)** $p = 60°$, $q = 30°$

5. a) 108° **b)** $x = 65°$

Page 59

1. See p.12 for diagrams

2. See p.12 for diagrams

3. a) 4 **b)** 2 **c)** 0 **d)** 2 **e)** 1 **f)** 0

4. See p.12 for diagrams. **a)** Order 4 **b)** Order 2 **c)** Order 1

5. a) See p.12 for diagram **b)** See p.12 for diagram. Order 6

6. a) 4 **b)** 2 **c)** 2 **d)** 2 **e)** 1 **f)** 1

Page 60

1. a) RHS **b)** SAS **c)** Not congruent **d)** SSS **e)** Not congruent
f) Not congruent **g)** ASA

2. a) DE = 7.5cm **b)** BD = 1.5cm

3. PQR and XYZ ASA

4. OA = OB radii, OÂB = OB̂A isosceles
AM = MB ∴ OM is a bisector
AMO = BMO
AMO + BMO = 180°
∴ AMO = BMO = 90°
∴ OM is a perpendicular bisector

5. ABC and XYZ similar, three corresponding angles.

Page 61

1. a) 13cm **b)** 7.2cm **c)** 16.4cm

2. $a^2 + b^2 = c^2$
$7.5^2 + 4^2 = 72.25$
$c = \sqrt{72.25} = 8.5cm$
Not 9.5cm. Triangle C is not a right angled triangle.

3. a) No **b)** Yes **c)** Yes **d)** Yes

4. 7.5cm

5. Yes, $6.25^2 − 6^2 = 1.75^2$ **or** $6^2 + 1.75^2 = 6.25^2$, etc.

6. 8.5cm
7. 9.5cm
8. a) 4.2m **b)** 3.2m
9. 11.4cm

Page 62
1. a) 5cm **b)** 11.3cm **c)** 13.2cm
2. a) 60° **b)** 41.8° **c)** 45°
3. $x = 15.1$cm
4. a) $5x$ **b)** $4x$ **c)** $\sqrt{32}x$ **d)** 27.9° **e)** 41.4°

Page 63
5. a) 7.15m **b)** 39.2°
6. a) 13cm **b)** 13.6cm **c)** 17.1°
7. a) 10cm, 9.43cm **b)** 26.6° **c)** 32.5°
8. 11.0m
9. a) 64.1° **b)** 63.4° **c)** 43.1cm
10. No, $\tan^{-1}(\frac{12.6}{6.3})$ does not equal 60°
11. a) 33.6m **b)** 2.7m
12. Height = 28cm, width = 24cm

Page 64
1. a) 6.8cm **b)** 7.5cm **c)** 9.4cm
2. a) 38.8° **b)** 57.1° **c)** 68.7°
3. a) 7.9cm **b)** 12.9cm **c)** 3.9cm

Page 65
4. a) 58.8° **b)** 50.3° **c)** 66.4°
5. a) 38.8° **b)** 251.2° **c)** 071.2° **d)** 45.3km
6. a) 41.9° **b)** 80.3m
7. a) 200.9m **b)** 192.6° **c)** 012.6°
8. a) 76.7° **b)** 48.4° **c)** 6.9m **d)** 62.2m²

Page 66
1. A centre, **B** Radius, **C** Diameter, **D** Circumference, **E** Chord, **F** Tangent
2. a) 45° **b)** 67.5°
3. a) See p.12 for diagram b) OTX and OWX, OTV and OWV, TVX and WVX **c)** 140°
4. a) Isosceles **b) i)** 20° **ii)** 20° **c) i)** 70° **ii)** 70° **iii)** 40° **d)** Isosceles
5. a) OX = 6.2m
b) AB and CD are parallel. OB, OD, OA, OC are all radii hence equal. Triangle OAC is congruent to triangle OBD hence AC = BD

Page 67
1. a) 124° Angles subtended by arc
b) 102° Angles subtended by arc
c) 90° Angles in semicircle
d) 74° Alternate segment
e) 86° Cyclic quadrilateral
f) 105° Angles in same segment
g) 45° Isosceles; angles in semicircle
h) 95° Alternate segment
i) 67° Angles subtended by arc
j) 36° Cyclic quadrilateral
k) 42° Angles in semicircle
l) 101° Angles in same segment

Page 68
2. a) $x = 30°$ Semicircle, $y = 30°$ Isosceles
b) $x = 40°$ Same segment, $y = 140°$ Same segment
c) $x = 40°$ Isosceles, $y = 20°$ Angles subtended by arc
3. a) 120° Semicircle and cyclic quadrilateral
b) 110° Straight line and cyclic quadrilateral
4. a) $x = 19$ **b)** $x = 33$
5. a)–e) Accept appropriate proofs

Page 69
1. See p.12 for diagrams
2. a) Parallelogram prism **b)** 8 **c) See p.12 for diagram d)** 1
3. a) and **d)** are correct nets
4. Accept any suitable construction, as long as all sides = 3cm. Hexagons can be anywhere as long as one is on the top and one is on the bottom of the main strip of squares. See p.12 for example.
5. 5
6. See p.12 for diagrams

Page 70
1. a) i) L **ii)** C **iii)** D **iv)** J **v)** G **vi)** H
b) Reflection in line $y = 2.5$
c) Reflection in $y = x$

2. A: Reflection in line $x = -2$ **B:** Reflection in line $y = x$
C: Reflection in line $y = -x$ **D:** Reflection in line $y = 0.5$
3. a)–c) See p.12 for grid

Page 71
1. a) i) F **ii)** H **iii)** C **iv)** I **v)** E **b)** 90° clockwise about origin
c) 270° clockwise about (-2,0)
2. See p.12 for grid
3. See p.12 for grid

Page 72
1. a) i) D **ii)** H **iii)** E **iv)** C **v)** I **vi)** J **b)** $\binom{-4}{-2}$ **c)** $\binom{8}{-4}$
2. See p.13 for grid
3. See p.13 for grid

Page 73
1. See p.13 for grid
2. a) Centre (-1,0) scale factor 2 **b)** Centre (15,1) scale factor $\frac{1}{2}$
3. See p.13 for grid

Page 74
1. See p.13 for grid
2. a) Enlargement, scale factor -2, centre (0,0)
b) Enlargement, scale factor -3, centre (-1,1)
c) Enlargement, scale factor $-\frac{1}{2}$, centre (-3,1)
3. a)–b) See p.13 for grid
c) i) Scale factor $-\frac{1}{3}$, centre (0,0) **ii)** Scale factor -2, centre (0,1)

Page 75
1. a) i) Reflection in y-axis **ii)** Reflection in x-axis
b) Rotation 180° about origin
2. a) i) Rotation clockwise 270° about origin (or 90° anticlockwise)
ii) Reflection in x-axis
b) Reflection line $y = x$
3. a–b) See p.13 for grid c) Rotation 180° about (1,1)
4. a–d) See p.13 for grid e) Rotation 180° about (2,0)
f) Reflection in line $y = x$

Page 76
1. a) $\vec{AB} = \binom{4}{2}$ $\vec{CD} = \binom{3}{-4}$ $\vec{EF} = \binom{2}{1}$ $\vec{GH} = \binom{-8}{-4}$ $\vec{IJ} = \binom{-7}{0}$ $\vec{KL} = \binom{4}{2}$ $\vec{MN} = \binom{0}{-2}$ $\vec{OP} = \binom{6}{3}$
b) i) Equal **ii)** $\vec{AB} = 2\vec{EF}$ **iii)** $\vec{AB} = -\frac{1}{2}\vec{GH}$ **iv)** $\vec{AB} = \frac{2}{3}\vec{OP}$
c) i) $\binom{7}{-2}$ **ii)** $\binom{1}{6}$ **iii)** $\binom{10}{5}$ **iv)** $\binom{16}{8}$ **v)** $\binom{-1}{3}$ **vi)** $\binom{0}{0}$ **vii)** $\binom{-7}{-2}$ **viii)** $\binom{-8}{-4}$
ix) $\binom{12}{6}$ **x)** $\binom{7}{-4}$
2. See p.13–14 for diagrams
3. a) $\binom{12}{-6}$ **b)** $\binom{-2}{1}$

Page 77
1. a) $-a + b$ **b)** $\frac{1}{2}a$ **c)** $-b + \frac{1}{2}a$
2. a) i) a **ii)** c **iii)** $\frac{1}{2}c$ **iv)** $\frac{1}{2}c$ **v)** $-a + \frac{1}{2}c$ **vi)** $-a + \frac{1}{2}c$
b) APCQ is parallelogram $\vec{AP}$ equal and parallel to $\vec{QC}$ $\vec{AQ}$ equal and parallel to $\vec{PC}$
3. a) i) $\frac{1}{3}a$ **ii)** $\frac{1}{3}c$ **iii)** $-\frac{1}{3}a + \frac{1}{3}c$ **iv)** $-\frac{2}{3}c$ **v)** $-\frac{2}{3}a$ **vi)** $\frac{2}{3}c - \frac{2}{3}a$
b) PXYQ is a trapezium, PQ parallel to XY
4. PS equal and parallel to QR, PS = QR = $-\frac{1}{2}\vec{AB} + \frac{1}{2}\vec{BC}$
SR equal and parallel to PQ, SR = PQ = $\frac{1}{2}\vec{BC} + \frac{1}{2}\vec{AB}$
5. a) $C\hat{A}G = H\hat{A}G$, $A\hat{C}B = A\hat{H}G$, $A\hat{B}C = A\hat{G}H$. Three matching angles = similar triangles
b) 1 : 4
6. See p.14 for grid
7. See p.14 for grid (3,0,3), (3,3,3), (0,3,3), (0,0,3)

Page 78
1–4. See p.14 for diagrams

Page 79
5. See p.14 for diagram
6. a) Accept any triangle that has bisectors crossing in the middle See p.14 for example
b) All angle bisectors intersect in middle
7. a) Accept suitable construction of an equilateral triangle of side 3cm b) Accept suitable construction of a square of side 6cm
8. Accept any suitable constructions

Page 80
1–4. See p.14 for diagrams

Page 81

1. a) 23.2cm b) 22.1cm c) 22.8cm d) 33.6cm e) 16cm f) 36cm

Page 82

2. 643cm
3. 45.1m
4. 410cm
5. 8.3cm
6. a) 75.4cm b) 7.5cm c) 37.7cm d) 376.8cm
7. a) 53.2cm b) 111.3cm

Page 83

1. a) 14cm² b) 13cm²
2. a) 1.08m² b) 75cm² c) 1.8cm² d) 264cm² e) 3550cm² f) 78.5cm²
3. a) 8.7cm² b) 18.8cm² c) 7.1cm² d) 19.5cm²

Page 84

4. 1.9m
5. 1.5m
6. a) 111cm² b) 0.8m²
7. a) 5.08cm² b) 82.8cm² c) 5.14cm²
8. a) 60°, 9.06cm² b) 106.3°, 11.2cm²
9. 4 × £4.99 = £19.96
10. a) 8.37cm b) 54.5cm c) 10.4cm

Page 85

1. a) 184cm² b) 105cm²
2. 534cm²
3. 201cm²
4. 24πm²
5. a) 616cm² b) 172cm² c) 314cm² d) 2460cm²
6. 36πcm²

Page 86

1. a) 81cm³ b) 785cm³ c) 30cm³
2. a) x = 2cm b) x = 6.25cm
3. 14 100cm³

Page 87

4. 31.4cm³
5. 39.5cm
6. 10.7cm
7. 74.2cm³
8. a) 628cm³ b) 6.4cm
9. 12.9cm

Page 88

1. a) See p.14 for diagram b) 29.2m – accept answers between 29m and 29.3m
2. a) 60km b) 24km c) Two from: Bodmin, Fowey, Holsworthy
3. a) See p.14 for diagram b) Approx. 94m
4. a) See p.14 for diagram b) Approx. 6.3m

Page 89

1. a) 4 : 9 b) 8 : 27
2. 125 : 512
3. a) 364.5cm² b) 21.3cm³
4. 21.56cm²
5. 754.6cm³
6. a) i) 15cm ii) 140.625cm³ b) i) 12cm ii) 48cm²
7. No, ratio height 22 : 33 or 2 : 3, ratio volume 8 : 27. A similar shape would have volume 455.625cm³

Page 90

1. a) 4.5m b) 3500ml c) 1250g d) 6.874kg e) 45 000m f) 5.5mm
2. a) 10.05m b) 1937m c) 2.65m
3. 4220mg, 0.405kg, 420g, 4kg, 39.5kg
4. a) 18 inches b) 180g c) 22.5 litres
5. Jake by 20cm
6. 1200m, 1 050 000mm, 1km, 900m, 11 000cm
7. a) 4.8km b) 7.5 miles c) 2025g d) 0.8 pounds e) 6.9 litres f) 39.4 pints
8. 11 000 yards
9. a) 4.6cm² b) 7600cm²
10. a) 0.5cm³ b) 30000cm³

Page 91

1. a) i) 090° ii) 047° iii) 125° iv) 227° v) 270° vi) 306°
   b) i) 351km ii) 50km iii) 30km
2. A → B = 045°, B → C = 145°, C → D = 215°, D → A = 308°

Page 91 (right column continued)

3. a) 238° b) 010° c) 126°
4. a) See p.14 for diagram b) 313°
5. See p.14 for diagram
6. See p.14 for diagram $x^2 = 15^2 + 12^2 - 2 \times 15 \times 12\cos160°$
   $x^2 = 707.28\ldots$
   BC = 26.6km

Page 92

1. 1.7 hours (1 d.p.) or 1 hour 40 mins
2. 11.2mph
3. 24m
4. 92.5km/h
5. 0.106g/cm³ or 106kg/m³
6. Volume = 500cm³, change by 50cm³
7. a) 108km/h b) 378km
8. a) 0.8g/cm³ b) 35 200g or 35.2kg

Page 93

1. a) i) $\frac{4}{10} = \frac{2}{5}$ ii) $\frac{3}{10}$ iii) $\frac{2}{10} = \frac{1}{5}$ iv) $\frac{1}{10}$ v) $\frac{6}{10} = \frac{3}{5}$ vi) $\frac{7}{10}$
   b) i)–iv)

   0   0.5   1
   D C B A
2. a) $\frac{4}{18} = \frac{2}{9}$ b) $\frac{14}{18} = \frac{7}{9}$ c) $\frac{5}{18}$ d) $\frac{13}{18}$ e) $\frac{9}{18} = \frac{1}{2}$ f) $\frac{9}{18} = \frac{1}{2}$
3. a) $\frac{1}{2}$ b) $\frac{1}{2}$ c) $\frac{10}{30} = \frac{1}{3}$ d) $\frac{22}{30} = \frac{11}{15}$ e) $\frac{8}{30} = \frac{4}{15}$
4. a) $\frac{2}{5}$ b) $\frac{3}{5}$ c) 0

Page 94

5. a) In any order: (2 of spades, 2 of diamonds) (2 of spades, 2 of hearts) (5 of spades, 2 of diamonds) (5 of spades, 2 of hearts)
   b) i) $\frac{2}{6} = \frac{1}{3}$ ii) $\frac{1}{6}$ iii) $\frac{5}{6}$
6. 0.3
7. 0.35
8. a) $\frac{8}{15}$ b) $\frac{1}{15}$
9. a) $\frac{7}{10}$ b) $\frac{3}{10}$ c) $\frac{3}{10}$ d) $\frac{7}{10}$ e) 1 f) 0
10. a) i) $\frac{3}{12} = \frac{1}{4}$ ii) $\frac{6}{12} = \frac{1}{2}$ iii) $\frac{2}{12} = \frac{1}{6}$ b) i) $\frac{9}{12} = \frac{3}{4}$ ii) $\frac{6}{12} = \frac{1}{2}$
    iii) $\frac{10}{12} = \frac{5}{6}$ c) 24

Page 95

1. a)

+	1	2	3	4	5	6
1	2	3	4	5	6	7
2	3	4	5	6	7	8
3	4	5	6	7	8	9
4	5	6	7	8	9	10
5	6	7	8	9	10	11
6	7	8	9	10	11	12

b) i) $\frac{6}{36} = \frac{1}{6}$ ii) $\frac{15}{36} = \frac{5}{12}$ iii) $\frac{15}{36} = \frac{5}{12}$ iv) $\frac{7}{36}$ v) 0
vi) $\frac{12}{36} = \frac{1}{3}$ vii) $\frac{12}{36} = \frac{1}{3}$

2. a)

+	1	1	2	10	20	20
1	2	2	3	11	21	21
2	3	3	4	12	22	22
5	6	6	7	15	25	25
5	6	6	7	15	25	25
10	11	11	12	20	30	30
50	51	51	52	60	70	70

b) i) $\frac{4}{36} = \frac{1}{9}$ ii) $\frac{3}{36} = \frac{1}{12}$ iii) $\frac{12}{36} = \frac{1}{3}$ iv) $\frac{6}{36} = \frac{1}{6}$ v) $\frac{5}{6}$ vi) 0

3. a)

	1	2	3	4	5	6
2	2	4	6	8	10	12
4	4	8	12	16	20	24
8	8	16	24	32	40	48
9	9	18	27	36	45	54
10	10	20	30	40	50	60

b) i) $\frac{2}{30} = \frac{1}{15}$ ii) $\frac{2}{30} = \frac{1}{15}$ iii) $\frac{9}{30} = \frac{3}{10}$ iv) $\frac{3}{30} = \frac{1}{10}$
v) $\frac{3}{30} = \frac{1}{10}$ vi) $\frac{27}{30} = \frac{9}{10}$

Page 96

1. a) $\frac{8}{15}$ b) $\frac{4}{5}$
2. a) $\frac{26}{52} = \frac{1}{2}$ b) $\frac{16}{52} = \frac{4}{13}$

3. **a)** $\frac{1}{36}$ **b)** $\frac{1}{4}$

4. $\frac{6}{90} = \frac{1}{15}$

5. **a)** $\frac{2}{15}$ **b)** $\frac{2}{10} = \frac{1}{5}$

6. **a)** $\frac{2}{182} = \frac{1}{91}$ **b)** $\frac{40}{182} = \frac{20}{91}$

Page 97

1. **a)** See p.14 for diagram **b) i)** 0.49 **ii)** 0.09 **iii)** 0.21 **iv)** 0.21 **v)** 0.42

2. **a)** 0.2 **b)** See p.14 for diagram **c) i)** 0.25
   ii) 0.09 + 0.06 + 0.06 + 0.04 = 0.25 **iii)** 0.06 **iv)** 0.62

3. **a)** See p.14 for diagram **b) i)** 0.64 **ii)** 0.32 **iii)** 0.04

Page 98

1. **a) i)** 60 **ii)** 40 **iii)** 20 **b) i)** 0.55 **ii)** 0.32 **iii)** 0.13

2. **a) i)** 0.44 **ii)** 0.53 **iii)** 0.46 **iv)** 0.48 **b)** See p.14 for graph

   c) 0.5 Theoretically $\frac{1}{2}$ landing on tails

3. **a)** 0.1, 0.08, 0.11, 0.13, 0.15, 0.16, 0.17, 0.18, 0.17, 0.16, 0.16, 0.16
   b) See p.14 for graph **c)** 246

Page 99

1. **a)** Interpret and discuss the data **b)** Process and represent the data, refine the question.

2. **a)–c)** Accept any suitable answers, e.g:
   Taking observations, e.g. Number of occupants in cars (Primary data);
   Results from an experiment (Primary data);
   A survey (Primary data);
   Records of historical data, e.g. weather conditions (Secondary data).

3. **A sensible answer will include:**
   a) Specify the problem and plan:
   Give your interpretation of the problem and define more precisely what you are trying to find out.
   Develop some outline ideas on how the data will be collected and how it might be used to provide the answers you are looking for.
   b) Decide what data to collect:
   Consider the various forms of exercise that pupils may take. Allow for others.
   Develop a data collection sheet that will provide the information that you need.
   c) Collect data from a variety of sources:
   Consider different primary sources. Decide whether secondary data may be used?
   d) Process and represent the data:
   Consider what calculations may be used with the data and how your results may be presented.
   e) Interpret and discuss the data:
   Decide what your results mean and try to come to some conclusions relating to your original interpretation of the problem.
   Consider further lines of inquiry.

4. **Accept any suitable answers, e.g:**
   Compare the performance of boys and girls in mathematics.
   Compare the height/weight of modern teenagers with those from, say, 50 years ago.
   Determine the influence that watching television has on performance in school.
   Consider the effectiveness of different training methods used for top athletes.
   Compare the music that young people like to listen to in different countries.
   You could use the data handling cycle to try to answer questions such as:
   • How much exercise do you need to stay healthy?
   • Does brain training make any difference?
   • In which sport do the competitors make most money?

Page 100

1. Primary data is obtained first hand usually by yourself. Secondary data is obtained from an external agency, e.g. data from the Internet.

2. **a)** Choosing a reliable, balanced group of people, ages, sex, etc.
   b) In a random sample individuals are selected arbitrarily. In a stratified sample individuals from different groups are selected in a specific ratio to reflect distribution within the population.
   c) No, should be taken from all over UK, males and females.

3. **a) i)** 30 students **ii)** 14 girls **b) i)** Year 7 **ii)** 20 boys, 16 girls

4. **a)** Not suitable – leading question **b)** Suitable – establishes if they eat breakfast **c)** Suitable – may not have time for breakfast **d)** Not suitable – not relevant **e)** Suitable – establishes age group **f)** Suitable – establishes what they eat **g)** Suitable – differences **h)** Not suitable – not relevant

Page 101

5. **a)** Accept any suitable questions **b)** Accept any variations, e.g. Do you agree we are the best supermarket?

6. **a)** Accept any suitable answer **b)** Accept any suitable answers, **e.g.** surveying pupils from different schools across all years.

7. A – 10, B – 25, C – 10, D – 5, E – 50

8. **a)** Accept any suitable answer
   b) Accept any suitable answer

9. **a)** Accept any suitable answer **b)** Accept any suitable answers, **e.g.** by asking girls and boys from all years.

Page 102

1. Discrete data can only take certain values. Continuous data can take any value (within a range), and is normally collected by measurement.

2. **Frequency:** 4, 7, 8, 12, 9, Total: 40

3. **a) Frequency:** 3, 5, 8, 13, 9, 2, Total: 40 **b)** 80%

Page 103

4. **Frequency:** 2, 3, 5, 9, 1, Total: 20

5. **a) Frequency:** 3, 12, 12, 3, Total: 30 **b)** 50%

6. **Frequency:** 11, 19, 5, 0, 3, Total: 38

7. **a)** Check correct class intervals have been used. **Frequency:** 1, 4, 8, 8, 4, 3, 2, Total: 30 **b)** 83.3̇%

8. Accept any appropriate class intervals, e.g.
   Weight: $50 \leqslant w < 55$, $55 \leqslant w < 60$, $60 \leqslant w < 65$, $65 \leqslant w < 70$, $70 \leqslant w < 75$, $75 \leqslant w < 80$, $80 \leqslant w < 85$, $85 \leqslant w < 90$, $90 \leqslant w < 95$,
   Frequency: 2, 1, 7, 3, 7, 8, 8, 3, 1, Total: 40

Page 104

1.
```
0 | 8 9
1 | 0 7
2 | 1 3 8 9
3 | 0 1 4 4 8
4 | 1 1 2 4 5 6 7 7
5 | 1 2 5 6 7 8
6 | 0 8
7 | 4
```
Key
1|7 = 17 years

2.

	Men	Women	Total
Listen to radio	32	41	73
Do not listen to radio	23	24	47
Total	55	65	120

3. **a)**

	Year 7	Year 8	Year 9	Total
Pop	42	30	18	90
Rap	16	12	13	41
Dance	14	24	31	69
Total	72	66	62	200

b) 45%

4. **a)**
```
16 | 4 6 7 9 9
17 | 0 1 1 3 3 3 4 4 5 5 6 8 8 8 8 9
18 | 0 1 2 4 6 8 9
19 | 1 2
```
Key
16|4 = 164 cm

b) $170 \leqslant h < 180$ **c)** 175.5cm

Page 105

1. **a)** 40 **b)** 1 **c)** 1 **d)** 4 **e)** 1.5

2. **a)** 24 **b)** 4 **c)** 3 **d)** 3

3. **a)**

Temp.	Freq.	Mid-temp	Freq. x Mid-temp
$5 \leqslant T < 10$	3	7.5	3 × 7.5 = 22.5
$10 \leqslant T < 15$	14	12.5	14 × 12.5 = 175
$15 \leqslant T < 20$	11	17.5	11 × 17.5 = 192.5
$20 \leqslant T < 25$	2	22.5	2 × 22.5 = 45

Estimated mean = 14.5

b) $10 \leqslant T < 15$ **c)** $10 \leqslant T < 15$

4. **a)** $\frac{563}{33} = 17.06$s **b)** $16 < T \leqslant 18$ **c)** $16 < T \leqslant 18$

Page 106

1. See p.14 for graph

2. **a)** See p.15 for diagram **b)** 35% **c)** $\frac{1}{10}$

3. **a)** Skimmed **b)** 1100 pints **c)** See p.15 for pictogram

Page 107
1. See p.15 for graph
2. a–b) See p.15 for graph c) Women generally spend more on cosmetics than men. Modal amount women $4 \leqslant M < 6$; Modal amount men $2 \leqslant M < 4$

Page 108
1. a) **Frequency Density:** 3, 4, 1.5, 2.5 b) See p.15 for graph
2. 23 students
3. a) Sales were probably greatest in December due to Christmas sales. b) Total sales to women 102 000; Total sales to men 100 000. Therefore he is incorrect.

Page 109
1. a) The longer the journey time the greater the distance travelled (positive correlation) b) **Accept a suitable line of best fit** c) i) Approx. 41.5 minutes ii) 1.6km
2. a) **See p.15 for graph** b) Positive correlation – as height increases weight increases c) i) Approx. 137cm ii) 86kg

Page 110
1. Accept any appropriate class intervals: a) **Temperature:** $15 \leqslant T < 20$, $20 \leqslant T < 25$, $25 \leqslant T < 30$, $30 \leqslant T < 35$, **Frequency:** 11, 13, 9, 7, Total: 40 b)–c) **See p.15 for graphs**
2. **See p.15 for graph**
3. a) **See p.15 for graph** b) The more chapters the more pages – positive c) i) Approx. 295 pages ii) Approx. 15 chapters
4. a) **See p.15 for diagram** b) 40%
5. a) i) 1.8 goals ii) 6 iii) 2 goals iv) 2 goals b) Year 10 by 1 goal
6. a) 17.1 sec b) $16 > t \leqslant 18$ c) $16 < t \leqslant 18$

Page 111
1. a) 8 b) 22 c) 43 mins
2. a) **Cumulative frequency:** 2, 6, 11, 18, 30, 35 b) **See p.15 for graph** c) i) Approx. 20 ii) 10 d) 19 e) 5 f) **See p.15 for box plot**

Page 112
3. a) **Cumulative frequency:** 10, 49, 144, 269, 300 b) **See p.15 for graph** c) i) Approx. 160cm ii) Approx. 12.5cm iii) Approx. 210
4. a) **See p.15 for graph** b) i) Approx. 70kg ii) Approx. 12 c) Approx. 52.5%

Answers to Graphs and Diagrams

Page 38, 11. a)

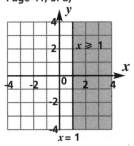

Page 38, 11. b)

```
      1                1
     1 1              1 1
    1 2 1            1 2 1
   1 3 3 1          1 3 3 1
  1 4 6 4 1        1 4 6 4 1
                  1 5 10 10 5 1
```

Page 39, 1.

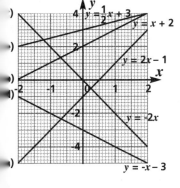

Page 39, 2. b)

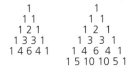
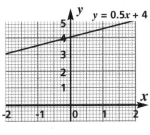

Page 39, 3. b)

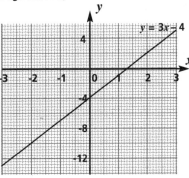

Page 39, 4. a)

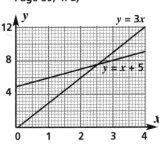

Page 41, 3. a)

Page 41, 3. b)

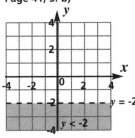

Page 41, 3. c)

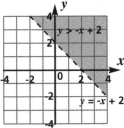

Page 41, 3. d)

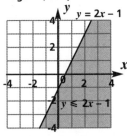

Page 42, 4. a)

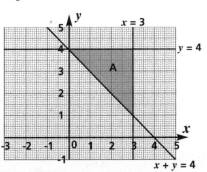

Page 42, 5. a)

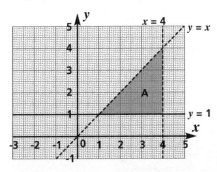

Page 42, 6.

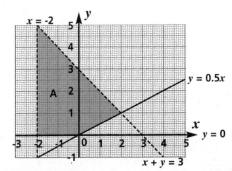

8

Page 42, 9.

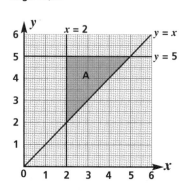

Page 42, 10.

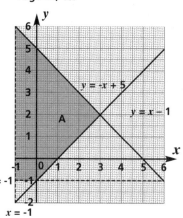

Page 44, 1. a)

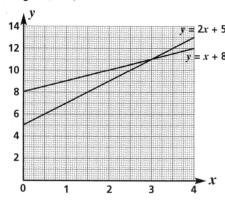

Page 44, 2. a)

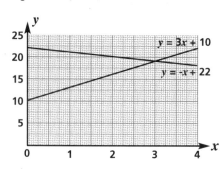

Page 44, 3. a)

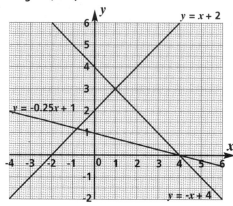

Page 44, 4. a)

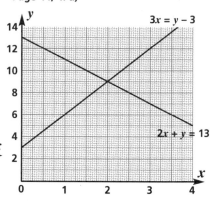

Page 44, 5. a)

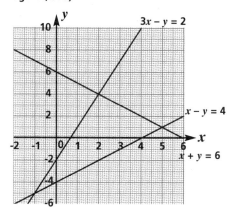

Page 46, 1. a)

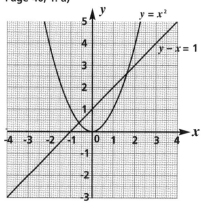

Page 46, 2. a)

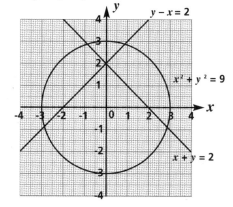

Page 46, 3. b) i)

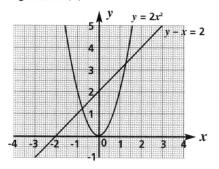

Page 46, 3. b) ii)

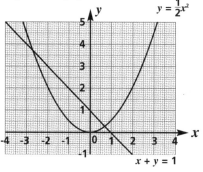

Page 46, 3. b) iii)

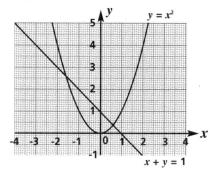

Page 46, 4. a)

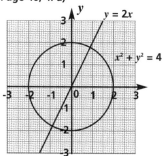

Page 46, 4. b)

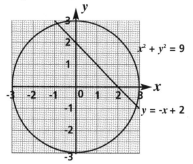

Page 46, 4. c)

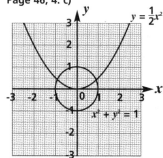

9

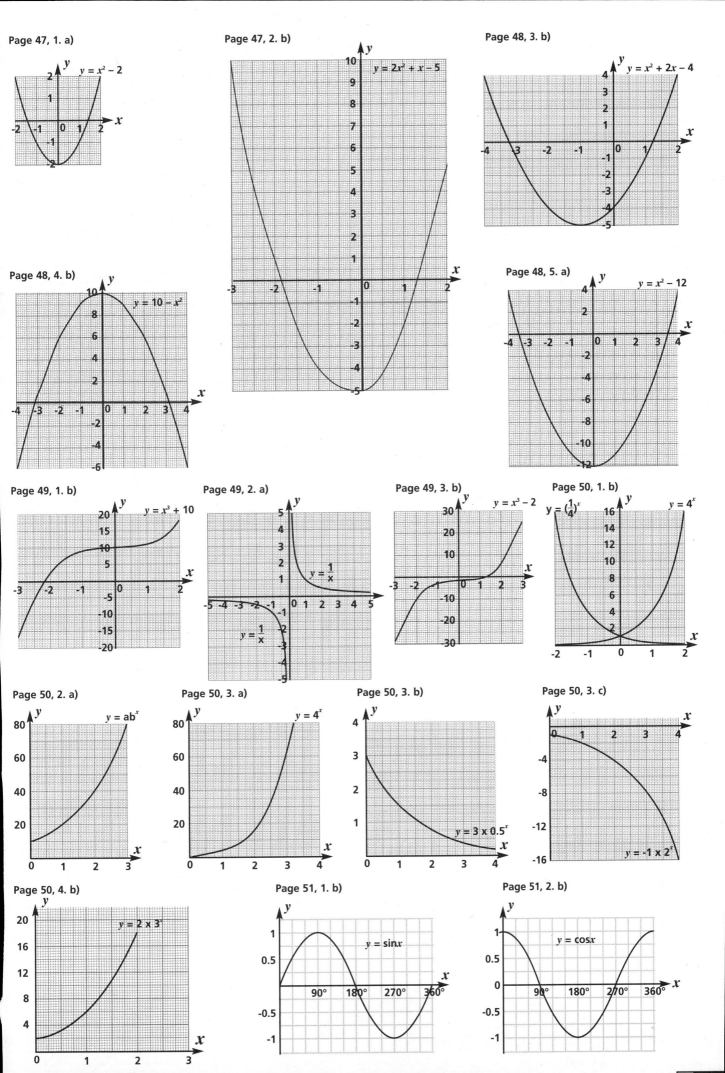

Page 47, 1. a)

$y = x^2 - 2$

Page 47, 2. b)

$y = 2x^2 + x - 5$

Page 48, 3. b)

$y = x^2 + 2x - 4$

Page 48, 4. b)

$y = 10 - x^2$

Page 48, 5. a)

$y = x^2 - 12$

Page 49, 1. b)

$y = x^3 + 10$

Page 49, 2. a)

$y = \frac{1}{x}$

$y = \frac{1}{x}$

Page 49, 3. b)

$y = x^3 - 2$

Page 50, 1. b)

$y = (\frac{1}{4})^x$

$y = 4^x$

Page 50, 2. a)

$y = ab^x$

Page 50, 3. a)

$y = 4^x$

Page 50, 3. b)

$y = 3 \times 0.5^x$

Page 50, 3. c)

$y = -1 \times 2^x$

Page 50, 4. b)

$y = 2 \times 3^x$

Page 51, 1. b)

$y = \sin x$

Page 51, 2. b)

$y = \cos x$

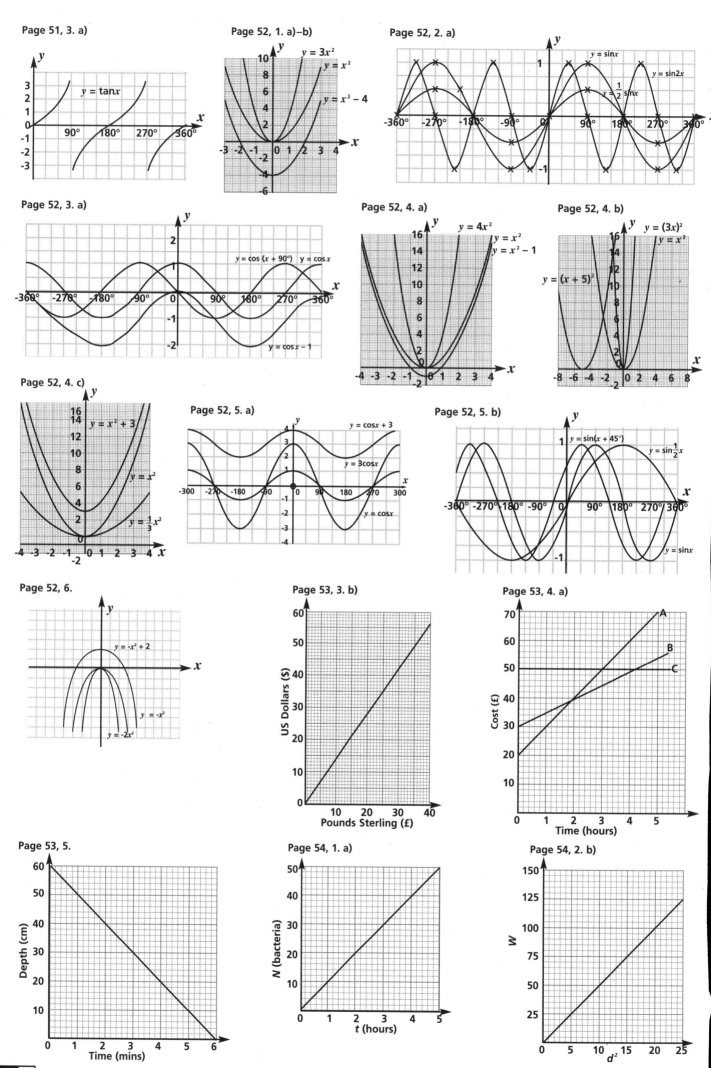

Page 51, 3. a)

Page 52, 1. a)–b)

Page 52, 2. a)

Page 52, 3. a)

Page 52, 4. a)

Page 52, 4. b)

Page 52, 4. c)

Page 52, 5. a)

Page 52, 5. b)

Page 52, 6.

Page 53, 3. b)

Page 53, 4. a)

Page 53, 5.

Page 54, 1. a)

Page 54, 2. b)

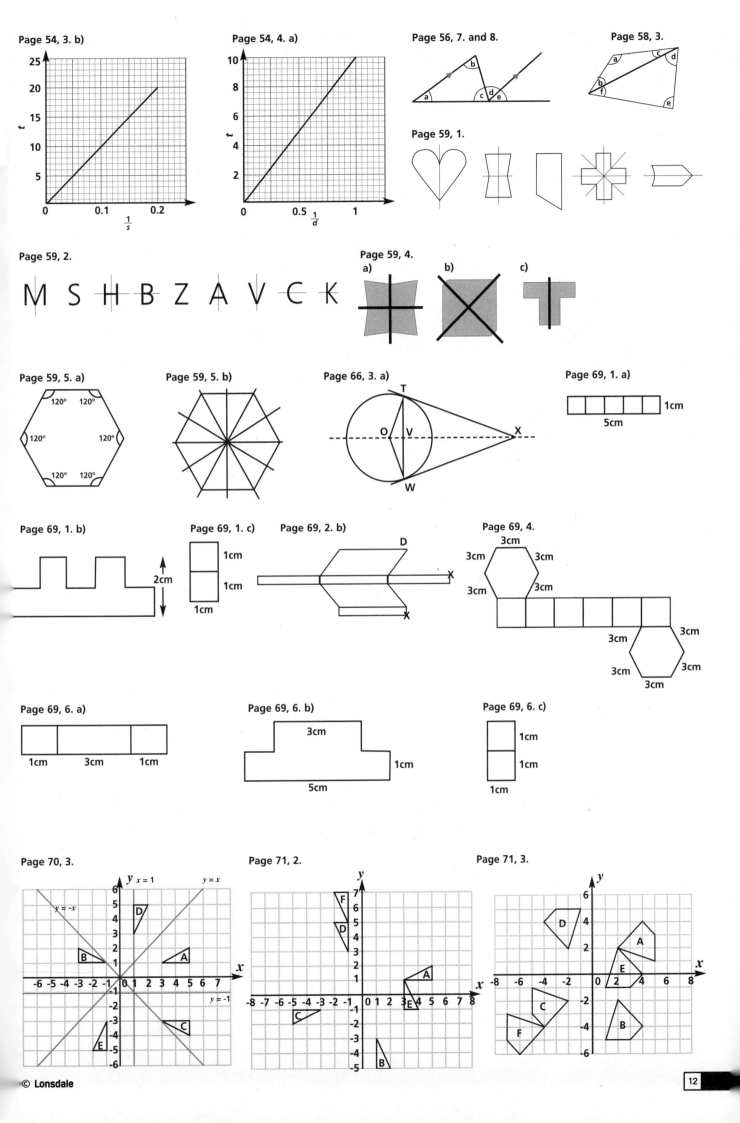

Page 54, 3. b)

Page 54, 4. a)

Page 56, 7. and 8.

Page 58, 3.

Page 59, 1.

Page 59, 2.

M S H B Z A V C K

Page 59, 4.

a)

b)

c)

Page 59, 5. a)

120° 120°
120°   120°
120° 120°

Page 59, 5. b)

Page 66, 3. a)

Page 69, 1. a)

5cm

1cm

Page 69, 1. b)

2cm

Page 69, 1. c)

1cm

1cm

1cm

Page 69, 2. b)

D

X

X

Page 69, 4.

3cm

3cm   3cm

3cm   3cm

3cm

3cm

3cm

3cm

3cm

3cm

Page 69, 6. a)

1cm   3cm   1cm

Page 69, 6. b)

3cm

1cm

5cm

Page 69, 6. c)

1cm

1cm

1cm

Page 70, 3.

Page 71, 2.

Page 71, 3.

Page 72, 2.

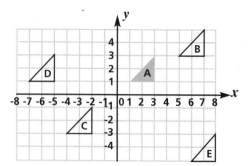

Page 72, 3.

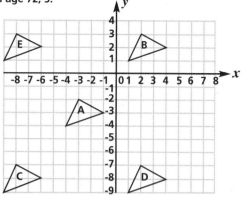

Page 73, 1.

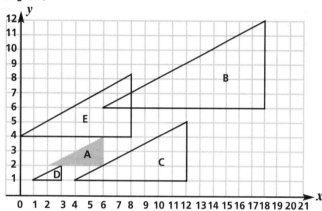

Page 73, 3.

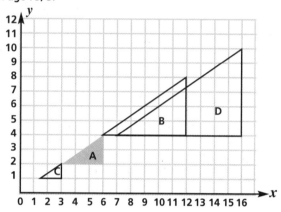

Page 74, 1.

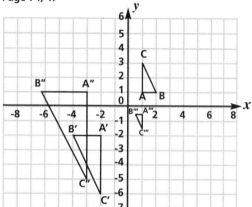

Page 74, 3.

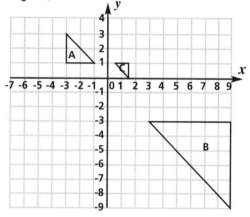

Page 75, 3. a)–b)

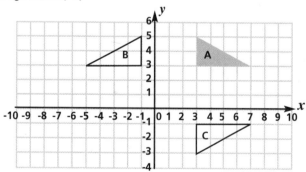

Page 75, 4. a)–d)

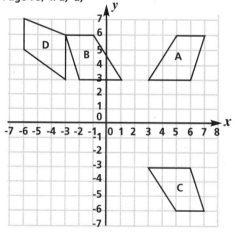

Page 76, 2. a)

Page 76, 2. b)

Page 76, 2. c)

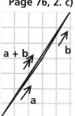

Page 76, 2. d)

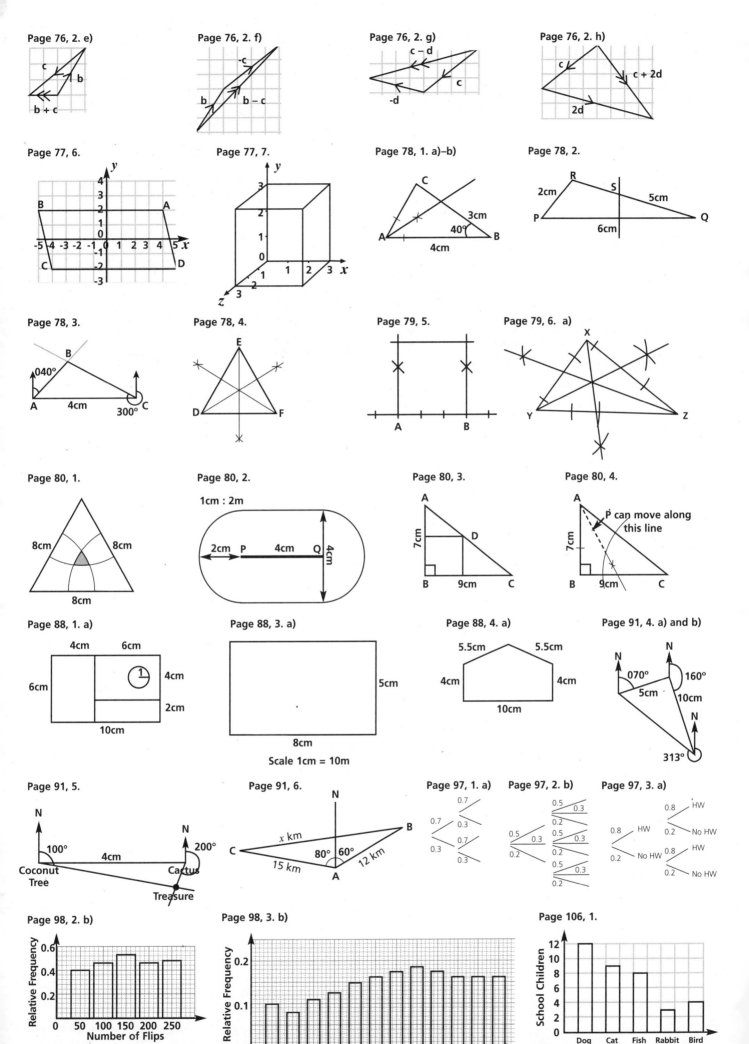

Page 76, 2. e)

Page 76, 2. f)

Page 76, 2. g)

Page 76, 2. h)

Page 77, 6.

Page 77, 7.

Page 78, 1. a)–b)

Page 78, 2.

Page 78, 3.

Page 78, 4.

Page 79, 5.

Page 79, 6. a)

Page 80, 1.

Page 80, 2.

Page 80, 3.

Page 80, 4.

Page 88, 1. a)

Page 88, 3. a)

Page 88, 4. a)

Page 91, 4. a) and b)

Page 91, 5.

Page 91, 6.

Page 97, 1. a)

Page 97, 2. b)

Page 97, 3. a)

Page 98, 2. b)

Page 98, 3. b)

Page 106, 1.

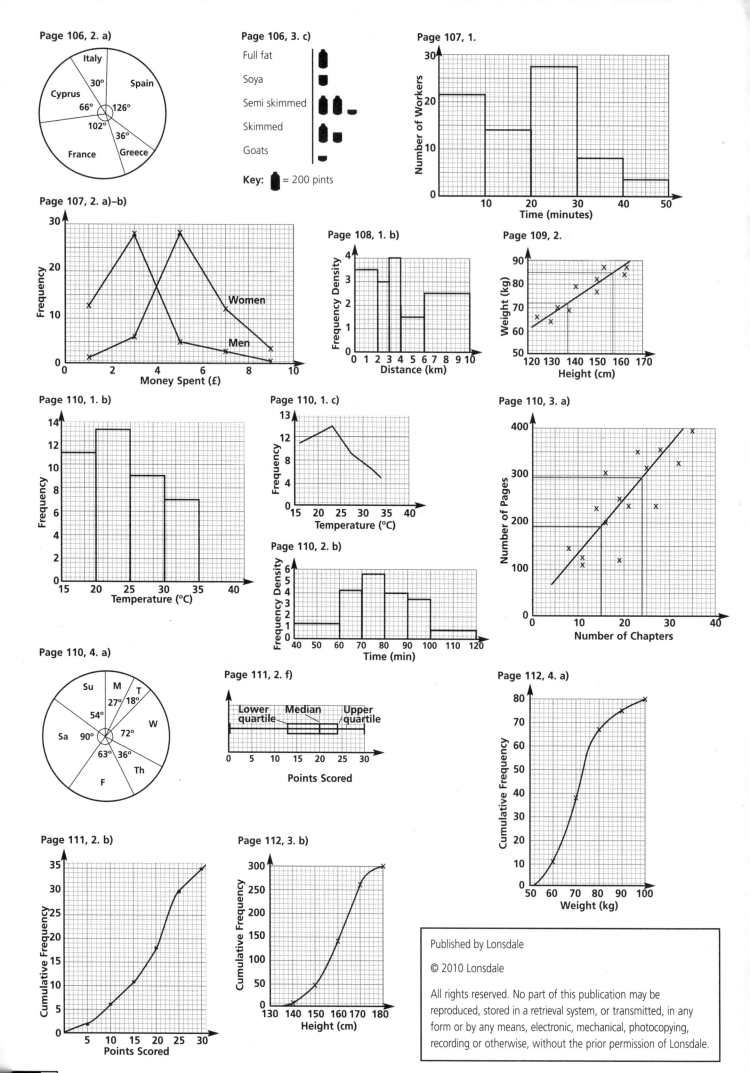

Page 106, 2. a)

Pie chart:
- Italy
- Spain 126°
- Cyprus 66°
- 30°
- France 102°
- Greece 36°

Page 106, 3. c)

Full fat
Soya
Semi skimmed
Skimmed
Goats

Key: = 200 pints

Page 107, 1.

Bar chart: Number of Workers vs Time (minutes)

Page 107, 2. a)–b)

Frequency vs Money Spent (£), Women and Men

Page 108, 1. b)

Frequency Density vs Distance (km)

Page 109, 2.

Weight (kg) vs Height (cm)

Page 110, 1. b)

Frequency vs Temperature (°C)

Page 110, 1. c)

Frequency vs Temperature (°C)

Page 110, 2. b)

Frequency Density vs Time (min)

Page 110, 3. a)

Number of Pages vs Number of Chapters

Page 110, 4. a)

Pie chart:
- Su
- M 27°
- T 18°
- W 72°
- Th 36°
- F 63°
- Sa 90°
- 54°

Page 111, 2. f)

Lower quartile, Median, Upper quartile — Points Scored

Page 112, 4. a)

Cumulative Frequency vs Weight (kg)

Page 111, 2. b)

Cumulative Frequency vs Points Scored

Page 112, 3. b)

Cumulative Frequency vs Height (cm)

Angles of Polygons

1 For each diagram below work out the size of angle p. They are not drawn to scale.

a)

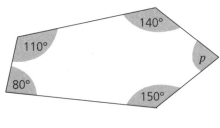

b)

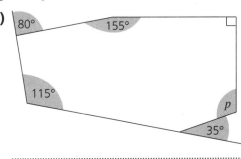

....

....

....

....

2 **a)** What do the exterior angles of an irregular pentagon add up to? ....

b) What do the exterior angles of a regular pentagon add up to? ....

3 An irregular polygon has exterior angles equal to 110°, 94°, 88° and 68°.

a) How many sides does the polygon have? ....

b) What is the sum of the interior angles of this irregular polygon?

....

....

4 An irregular polygon has interior angles equal to 110°, 155°, 135°, 95°, 140° and 85°.

a) How many sides does the polygon have? ....

b) What is the sum of the exterior angles of this irregular polygon?

....

....

5 An irregular pentagon has four exterior angles equal to 47°, 113°, 55° and 71°. What is the size of the fifth exterior angle?

....

6 A polygon has interior angles equal to x°, $x + 20$°, $2x$°, $2x - 10$° and 50°.
  a) How many sides does this polygon have?
  b) Work out the size of x.
  c) What is the size of each exterior angle?

7 A regular polygon has each interior angle equal to $1\frac{1}{2}$ times each exterior angle.
  a) What is the size of each interior angle?
  b) What is the size of each exterior angle?
  c) How many sides does this regular polygon have?

8 A regular polygon has each interior angle equal to 170°. How many sides does it have?

Quadrilaterals

 1 Below are four quadrilaterals. For each quadrilateral work out the missing angle x and name the type of quadrilateral, giving a reason for your answer. They are not drawn to scale.

a)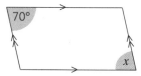

b)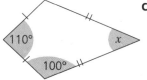

c)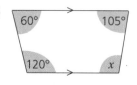

d)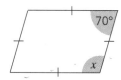

Angle x = ...

Type of Quadrilateral:

....

Reason:

....

....

Angle x = ...

Type of Quadrilateral:

....

Reason:

....

....

Angle x = ...

Type of Quadrilateral:

....

Reason:

....

....

Angle x = ...

Type of Quadrilateral:

....

Reason:

....

....

2 Read each sentence and name the quadrilateral described.

a) I have diagonals that are not equal in length but they bisect each other at right-angles.

....

b) I have diagonals that are equal in length and bisect each other. However, they do not bisect each other at right-angles.

....

c) I have diagonals that are equal in length and bisect each other at right-angles.

....

3 Draw a diagram and write a short explanation to prove that the interior angles of a quadrilateral add up to 360°.

....

....

4 Calculate the size of the labelled angles in the following diagrams. They are not drawn to scale.

a)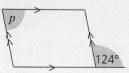

b)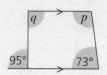

c)

d)

5 **a)** The interior angles of a quadrilateral are $x°$, $2x°$, $3x°$ and $4x°$. Work out the difference in size between the largest angle and the smallest angle in the quadrilateral.

b) The interior angles of a quadrilateral in degrees are $x + 20°$, $x - 30°$, $2x°$ and $110°$. Work out the size of x.

Symmetry

1 Draw all the lines of symmetry for each of the following shapes.

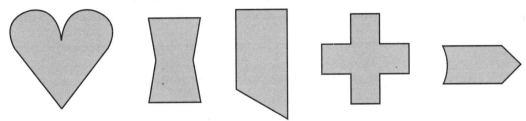

2 Mark on the lines of symmetry for each of these letters.

M S H B Z A V C K

3 How many lines of symmetry do each of the following quadrilaterals have?

a) Square ☐ ....

b) Rectangle ▭ ....

c) Parallelogram ▱ ....

d) Rhombus ▱ ....

e) Kite ◁ ....

f) Trapezium ◿ ....

4 For each of the following shapes draw all the lines of symmetry and write down the order of rotational symmetry for each shape.

a)

b)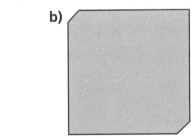

c)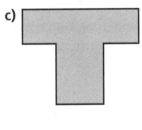

Order of rotational symmetry:

....

Order of rotational symmetry:

....

Order of rotational symmetry:

....

5 **a)** Draw a regular hexagon. Interior angles are 120°.

b) Draw all the lines of symmetry and write down the order of rotational symmetry.

6 **Write down the order of rotational symmetry for each quadrilateral:**

a) Square **b)** Rectangle **c)** Parallelogram **d)** Rhombus **e)** Kite **f)** Trapezium.

Congruence and Similarity

1 Which of the following pairs of triangles, A and B, are congruent? For each pair that is congruent, give the reason why, e.g. SAS, SSS, ASA, RHS. They are not drawn to scale.

a)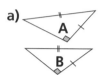

....

b)

....

c)

....

d)

....

e)

....

f)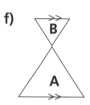

....

g)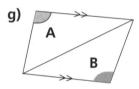

....

2 In the diagram below, BC is parallel to DE. AB = 3cm, AC = 4cm, BC = 5cm and CE = 2cm. The diagram is not drawn to scale.

a) Calculate the length of DE

....

b) Calculate the length of BD

....

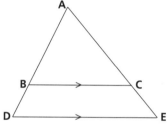

3 Here are three triangles (not drawn to scale). Which two triangles are congruent? Explain your answer.

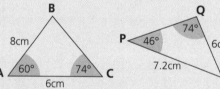

4 Using congruent triangles, prove that the line drawn from the centre of a circle through the midpoint of a chord is the perpendicular bisector of the chord.

5 Here are three triangles (not drawn to scale). Which two triangles are similar? Explain.

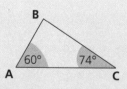 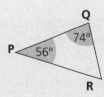 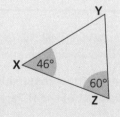

Pythagoras' Theorem

1 Use Pythagoras' theorem to calculate the unknown side in each of the following triangles.

They are not drawn to scale. If need be, give your answer to 1 decimal place.

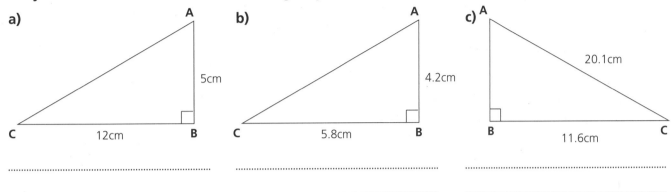

a)

A

5cm

C   12cm   B

b)

A

4.2cm

C   5.8cm   B

c) A

20.1cm

B   11.6cm   C

....

....

....

....

....

....

2 Which of the following triangles is not a right-angled triangle? Show all your workings.

They are not drawn to scale.

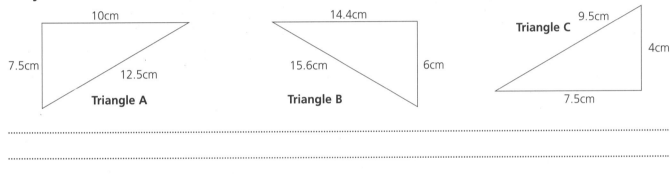

10cm

7.5cm

12.5cm

Triangle A

14.4cm

15.6cm   6cm

Triangle B

9.5cm

Triangle C   4cm

7.5cm

....

....

....

3 Would the following triangles be right angled?
  a) a = 2   b = 3   c = 4   b) a = 5   b = 12   c = 13
  c) a = 9   b = 12   c = 15   d) a = 1.2   b = 1.6   c = 2

4 The diagram shows a triangular prism.
  Calculate the length of CE. Give your answer to 2 significant figures.

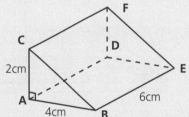

F

C   D

2cm   E

A   6cm

4cm   B

5 Triangle ABC has AB = 1.75cm, BC = 6cm and AC = 6.25cm. Is triangle
  ABC a right-angled triangle? Explain your answer.

6 A square has an area of 36cm². Calculate the length of its diagonal to 1 decimal place.

7 A rectangle has an area of 36cm² and the length of its base is twice that of its height.
  Calculate the length of its diagonal.

8 A 4.5m ladder leans against a wall. The foot of the ladder is 1.5m from the base of the wall.
  a) How high up the wall does the ladder reach? Give your answer to 1 decimal place.
  b) The position of the ladder is now changed so that the distance from the foot of the ladder to the base of the wall is the
      same as the distance the ladder reaches up the wall. How high up the wall does the ladder now reach, to 1 decimal place?

9 The length of the diagonal of a rectangle is 12cm. The length of its base is three times that of its height.
  Calculate the length of the base.

Trigonometry

1 Use trigonometry to calculate the length of...

a) BC

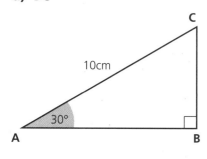

b) AB to 3 significant figures

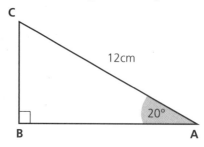

c) AB to 1 decimal place.

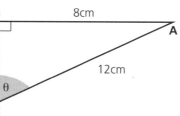

....

....

2 Use trigonometry to calculate the size of angle θ in the following triangles. If need be, give your answer to 1 decimal place.

a)

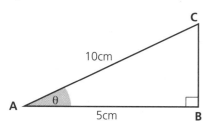

b)

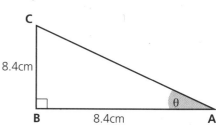

c)

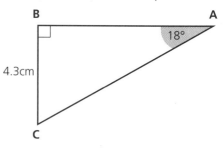

....

....

3 Calculate *x* to 1 d.p.

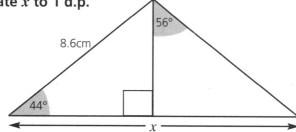

....

....

....

....

4 The diagram shows a cuboid. AB = DC = EF = HG = 3*x*,
BC = AD = FG = EH = 4*x* and AE = BF = CG = DH = $\sqrt{7}x$.

a) Calculate the length of AC in terms of *x*.

b) Calculate the length of AF in terms of *x*.

c) Calculate the length of AG in terms of *x*. Leave your answer in surd form.

d) Calculate the angle that line AG makes with the horizontal base ABCD (to 1 d.p.).

e) Calculate the angle that line AF makes with the horizontal base ABCD (to 1 d.p.).

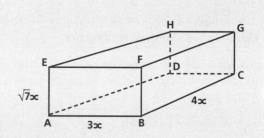

Trigonometry

5 **The tree in the diagram is 4.2m high. From A the angle of elevation to the top of the tree is 30.4°.**

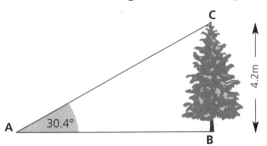

a) Calculate the distance from A to the base of the tree, B, to 2 decimal places.

....

....

....

b) The angle of elevation of the tree is now measured from a position 2m closer to the tree. Calculate the angle of elevation, to 1 decimal place.

....

....

....

6 **The diagram shows a rectangular box. Find...**

a) AC ....

b) AG ....

c) the angle between AC and AG. ....

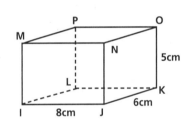

7 **The diagram shows a cuboid. Calculate...**

a) the lengths LJ and MJ ....

b) the angle between PJ and the plane IJKL. ....

c) the angle between MK and the plane MNIJ. ....

8 **The angle of depression from the top of one vertical pole to the top of another vertical pole is 24.5°. The height of one pole is 20m and the other is 15m. How far apart are the poles to 1 decimal place?**

9 **Triangle ABC is a right-angled triangle with BÂC = 90°. Use trigonometry to calculate the following:**
a) Angle ABC to 1 decimal place if AB = 70cm and BC = 1.6m.
b) Angle ABC to 1 decimal place if the length of AC is twice the length of AB.
c) The length of AB to 1 decimal place if AC = 14cm and angle ACB is four times the size of angle ABC.

10 **Triangle ABC has AB = 12.6cm, BC = 6.3cm and angle ACB = 60°.**
Is triangle ABC a right-angled triangle? Explain your answer.

11 a) The angle of elevation of the top of a tower from a point 30m away from the foot of the tower is 48.2°. Calculate the height of the tower to 1 decimal place.
b) The tower has a flag and the angle of elevation of the top of the flag from the same point is 50.4°. Calculate the height of the flag to 1 decimal place.

12 **The diagram (not drawn to scale) shows a picture hanging on a wall. AD = 3m, AB = 1.4m and CD = 1.8m. Calculate the height and width of the picture (to 1 d.p).**

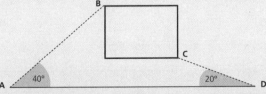

Trigonometry

For questions 1 and 2 use the sine rule only and give your answers to 1 decimal place.

The triangles are not drawn to scale.

1 a) Calculate BC

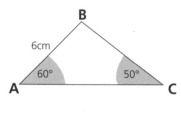

....

....

....

....

b) Calculate AB

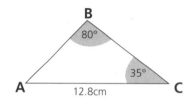

....

....

....

....

c) Calculate AC

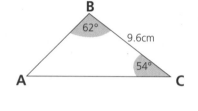

....

....

....

....

2 a) Calculate AĈB

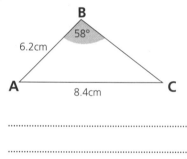

....

....

....

....

b) Calculate AB̂C

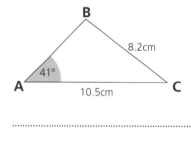

....

....

....

....

c) Calculate BÂC

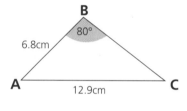

....

....

....

....

For questions 3 and 4 use the cosine rule only and give your answers to 1 decimal place.

The triangles are not drawn to scale.

3 a) Calculate BC

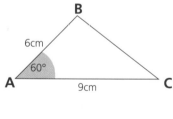

....

....

....

....

b) Calculate AC

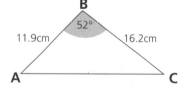

....

....

....

....

c) Calculate AB

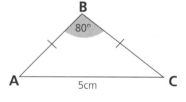

....

....

....

....

Trigonometry

4 a) Calculate B$\hat{A}$C

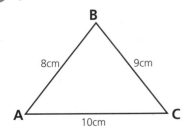

B

8cm   9cm

A   C
      10cm

....
....
....
....

b) Calculate A$\hat{B}$C

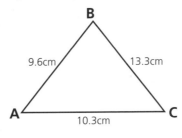

B

9.6cm   13.3cm

A   C
      10.3cm

....
....
....
....

c) Calculate A$\hat{C}$B

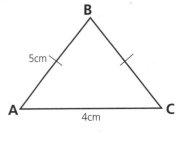

B

5cm

A   C
      4cm

....
....
....
....

5 A ship sails from Point A due north for 30km to reach Point B. The ship then changes course and sails on a bearing of 110° to reach Point C, which is 45km from Point A, as shown in the diagram.

a) Calculate B$\hat{C}$A. Give your answer to 1 decimal place.

....
....
....

b) Calculate the bearing of A from C.

....

c) Calculate the bearing of C from A.

....

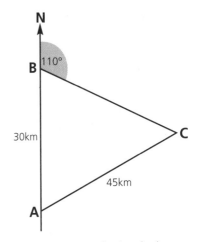

N

B 110°

30km

A

45km

C

d) Calculate the distance BC to 1 decimal place.

....
....

6 The direct distance from a post office, P, to a shop, S, is 100m and to a newsagent, N, is 67m. If S$\hat{N}$P = 85°, calculate: **a)** P$\hat{S}$N **b)** the distance from the shop to the newsagent. Give your answers to 1 decimal place.

7 Three girls, Alex, Bella and Carrie, stand at three points. The bearing of Bella from Alex is 075° and the bearing of Carrie from Alex is 143°. The distance from Alex to Bella is 165m and the distance from Alex to Carrie is 192m. Calculate: **a)** the distance from Bella to Carrie **b)** the bearing of Carrie from Bella **c)** the bearing of Bella from Carrie. Give your answers to 1 decimal place.

8 The diagram (not drawn to scale) shows the end wall of a house. If the distance from B to D is 6.9m, calculate: **a)** B$\hat{C}$D **b)** C$\hat{B}$D **c)** the distance AE **d)** the area of the end wall section of the house. Give your answers to 1 decimal place.

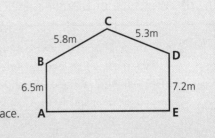

C
5.8m   5.3m
B   D
6.5m   7.2m
A   E

Circles

1 **Name each of the parts of the circle labelled A to F opposite.**

A .... B ....

C .... D ....

E .... F ....

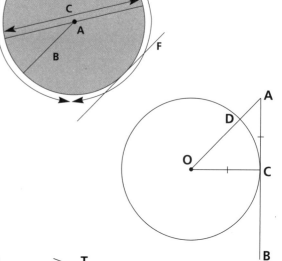

2 **In the diagram opposite, O is the centre of the circle.**
AB is a tangent touching the circle at C.
OC = AC. Find the size of...

a) angle COA ....

b) angle ODC ....

3 **XT and XW are tangents touching the circle at T and W.**

a) Draw the axis of symmetry in OTXW.

b) Name three pairs of congruent triangles.

....

c) If angle TXW is 40°, what is angle TOW?

....

4 **In the diagram opposite, O is the centre of the circle and PQ and PR are tangents.**

a) What name is given to triangle OQR? ....

b) Find the size of angle...

   i) OQR ....

   ii) ORQ ....

c) Find the size of angle...

   i) RQP ....

   ii) QRP ....

   iii) QPR ....

d) What type of triangle is PQR? ....

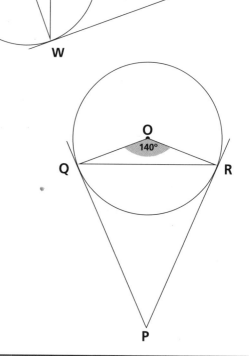

5 **a)** In diagram A, calculate the length OX (to 1 d.p.) if the chord is 10m long and radius OW is 8m long.

b) In diagram B, AB and CD are parallel chords. OPQ is perpendicular to AB and CD. Explain why AC = BD.

Diagram A

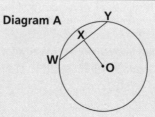

Diagram B

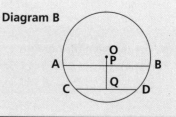

Circles

1 Find the size of x. Give a reason for your answer. The diagrams are not drawn to scale.

a)

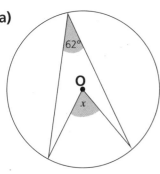

....

....

b)

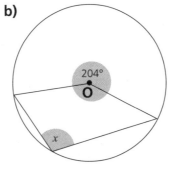

....

....

c)

....

....

d)

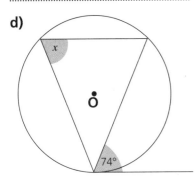

....

....

e)

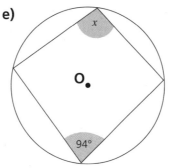

....

....

f)

....

....

g)

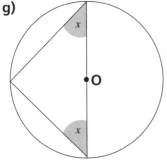

....

....

h)

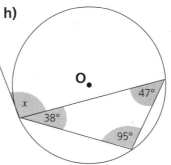

....

....

i)

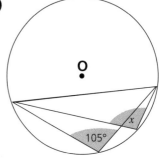

....

....

j)

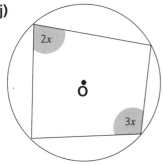

....

....

k)

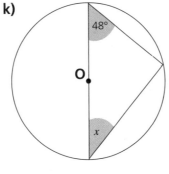

....

....

l)

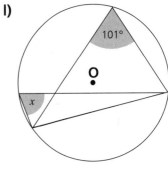

....

....

Circles

2 Find the size of x and y. Give a reason for your answer. The diagrams are not drawn to scale.

a)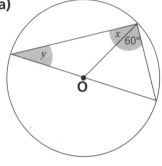

b)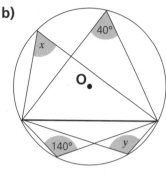

c)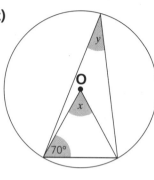

....

....

3 Find the size of angle AED. Give a reason for your answer. The diagrams are not drawn to scale.

a)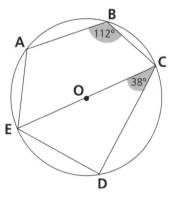

b)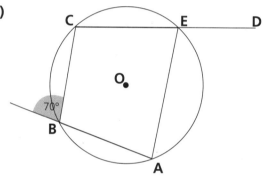

....

....

4 Calculate the value of x. The diagrams are not drawn to scale.

a)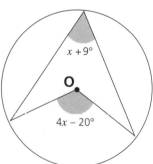

b)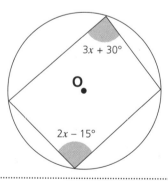

....

....

5 By means of a suitable diagram prove the following:

a) The angle subtended by a semicircle is 90°.   **b)** Opposite angles of a cyclic quadrilateral add up to 180°.

c) The angle subtended between a tangent to a circle and its chord is equal to the angle subtended in the alternate segment.

d) Angles subtended by an arc are equal in size.   **e)** Angles subtended in the same segment are equal in size.

1 The diagram shows a solid. Draw and label an accurate diagram

of the solid showing...

a) plan view b) front elevation c) side elevation

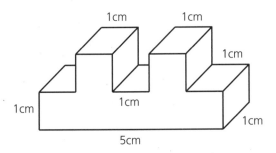

a)

b)

c)

2 A net of a solid is shown opposite.

a) What is the name of the 3-D solid?

....

b) How many vertices does it have?

....

c) Which other corners meet at D? Put an X on each one.

....

d) How many planes of symmetry does the solid have?

....

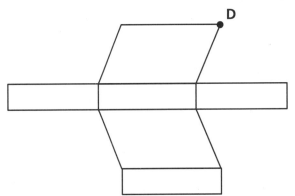

3 Which of the following are nets for a triangular prism? Place a tick beside the correct net(s).

a)

b)

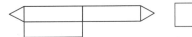

c)

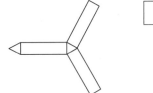

d)

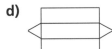

4 Draw an accurate full-size net of a regular hexagonal prism
with each edge 3cm long.

5 How many planes of symmetry does a cube have?

6 Draw the a) plan b) front elevation c) side elevation of this solid.

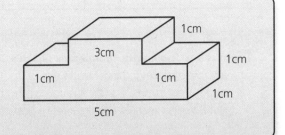

Transformations

1 **The grid shows twelve shapes A to L.**

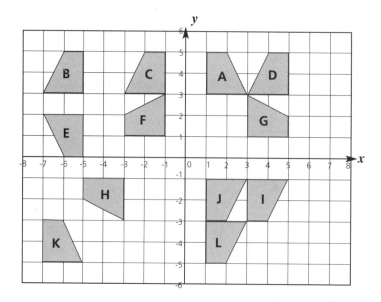

a) Which image shows object A reflected in the following?

   i) In the x-axis .... **ii)** In the y-axis .... **iii)** In the line $x = 3$ ....

   iv) In the line $y = 1$ .... **v)** In the line $y = x$ .... **vi)** In the line $y = -x$ ....

b) Describe the single reflection that takes B to E. ....

c) Describe the single reflection that takes F to J. ....

2 **Triangles A, B, C and D are all different reflections of the black triangle. For each one give the equation of the mirror line.**

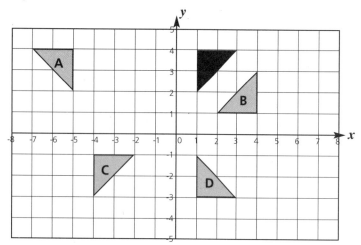

Triangle A: ....

....

Triangle B: ....

....

Triangle C: ....

....

Triangle D: ....

....

3 **A is a triangle with coordinates (3,1), (5,1) and (5,2).**

   a) On a suitable grid draw triangle A.

   b) i) Reflect triangle A in the line $x = 1$. Label this triangle B. **ii)** Reflect triangle A in the line $y = -1$. Label this triangle C.

      iii) Reflect triangle A in the line $y = x$. Label this triangle D. **iv)** Reflect triangle A in the line $y = -x$. Label this triangle E.

Transformations

1 **The grid shows ten shapes A to J.**

a) Take shape A as the object and name its image under each of these rotations.

i) 90° clockwise about the origin (0,0)

....

ii) 180° about the origin (0,0)

....

iii) 270° clockwise about the origin (0,0)

....

iv) 90° clockwise about the centre (-2,0)

....

v) 180° about the centre (-1,1)

....

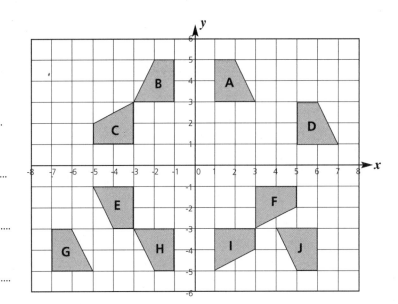

b) Describe the single rotation that takes C to A. ....

c) Describe the single rotation that takes I to A. ....

2 **The grid shows triangle A.**

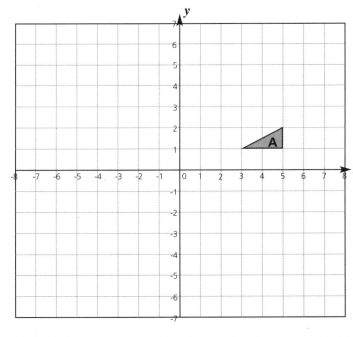

a) Rotate triangle A 90° clockwise about the origin (0,0). Label this triangle B.

b) Rotate triangle A 180° about the origin (0,0). Label this triangle C.

c) Rotate triangle A 270° clockwise about the origin (0,0). Label this triangle D.

d) Rotate triangle A 90° clockwise about the centre (3,1). Label this triangle E.

e) Rotate triangle A 270° clockwise about the centre (-1,1). Label this triangle F.

3 **A is a quadrilateral with coordinates (2,2), (4,4), (5,3) and (5,1).**

a) On a suitable grid draw quadrilateral A.

b) i) Rotate quadrilateral A 90° clockwise about the origin (0,0). Label this quadrilateral B. **ii)** Rotate quadrilateral A 180° about the origin (0,0). Label this quadrilateral C. **iii)** Rotate quadrilateral A 270° clockwise about the origin (0,0). Label this quadrilateral D. **iv)** Rotate quadrilateral A 90° clockwise about the centre (2,2). Label this quadrilateral E. **v)** Rotate quadrilateral A 180° about the centre (-1,-1). Label this quadrilateral F.

Transformations

1 The grid shows ten triangles A to J.

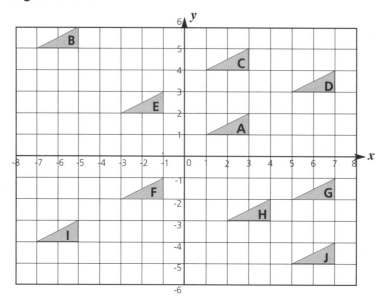

a) Name the image of triangle A under the translation given by each of the following vectors:

i) $\begin{pmatrix} 4 \\ 2 \end{pmatrix}$ ....

ii) $\begin{pmatrix} 1 \\ -4 \end{pmatrix}$ ....

iii) $\begin{pmatrix} -4 \\ 1 \end{pmatrix}$ ....

iv) $\begin{pmatrix} 0 \\ 3 \end{pmatrix}$ ....

v) $\begin{pmatrix} -8 \\ -5 \end{pmatrix}$ ....

vi) $\begin{pmatrix} 4 \\ -6 \end{pmatrix}$ ....

b) What is the translation vector that maps triangle D onto triangle A? ....

c) What is the translation vector that maps triangle B onto triangle A? ....

2 The grid shows triangle A. Draw and label the images described by these translations.

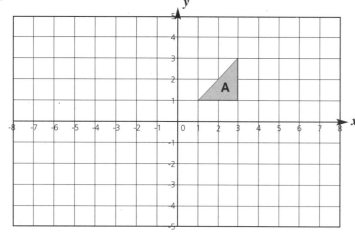

a) Triangle A mapped onto triangle B by the translation vector $\begin{pmatrix} 4 \\ 2 \end{pmatrix}$

b) Triangle A mapped onto triangle C by the translation vector $\begin{pmatrix} -5 \\ -4 \end{pmatrix}$

c) Triangle A mapped onto triangle D by the translation vector $\begin{pmatrix} -8 \\ 0 \end{pmatrix}$

d) Triangle A mapped onto triangle E by the translation vector $\begin{pmatrix} 5 \\ -6 \end{pmatrix}$

3 A is a triangle with coordinates (-1,-3), (-3,-2) and (-4,4).
a) On a suitable grid draw triangle A.
b) i) Translate triangle A by the vector $\begin{pmatrix} 5 \\ 5 \end{pmatrix}$ Label this triangle B. **ii)** Translate triangle A by the vector $\begin{pmatrix} -5 \\ -5 \end{pmatrix}$ Label this triangle C.

iii) Translate triangle A by the vector $\begin{pmatrix} 5 \\ -5 \end{pmatrix}$ Label this triangle D. **iv)** Translate triangle A by the vector $\begin{pmatrix} -5 \\ 5 \end{pmatrix}$ Label this triangle E.

Transformations

1 **The grid shows triangle A.**

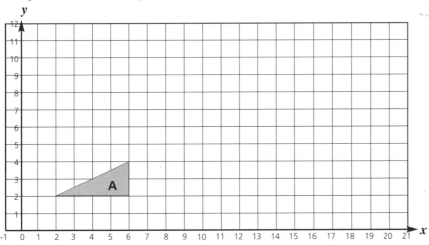

Enlarge triangle A by...

a) a scale factor of 3 about the centre of enlargement (0,0). Label this triangle B.

b) a scale factor of 2 about the centre of enlargement (0,3). Label this triangle C.

c) a scale factor of $\frac{1}{2}$ about the centre of enlargement (0,0). Label this triangle D.

d) a scale factor of 2 about the centre of enlargement (4,0). Label this triangle E.

2 **The grid shows three quadrilaterals A, B and C.**

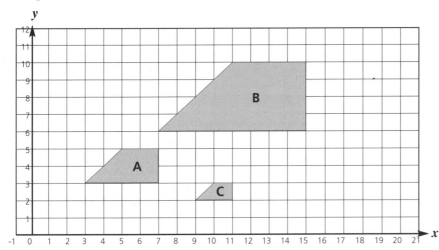

Describe fully the enlargement that would map quadrilateral A...

a) onto B. ....

b) onto C. ....

3 **Triangle A has coordinates (3,2), (6,2) and (6,4).**
   a) On a suitable grid draw triangle A.
   b) Complete the following enlargements: **i)** Triangle A is enlarged by a scale factor of 2, centre of enlargement (0,0).
   Label this triangle B. **ii)** Triangle A is enlarged by a scale factor of $\frac{1}{2}$, centre of enlargement (0,0). Label this triangle C.
   iii) Triangle A is enlarged by a scale factor of 3, centre of enlargement (1,1). Label this triangle D.

Transformations

1 On the axes below, draw the enlargement of triangle ABC by the following scale factors.

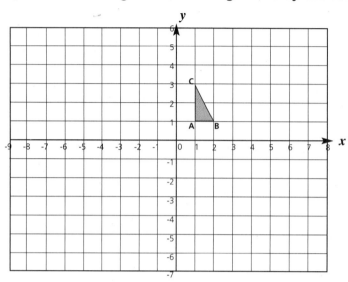

a) Scale factor -2, centre (0,0). Label this triangle A'B'C'.

b) Scale factor -3, centre (0,1). Label this triangle A"B"C".

c) Scale factor -$\frac{1}{2}$, centre (1,0). Label this triangle A'''B'''C'''.

2 The grid shows four triangles, P, Q, R and S.

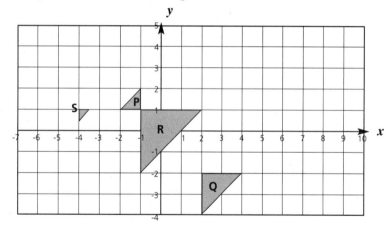

Describe fully the transformation that maps triangle P onto...

a) Q ....

b) R ....

c) S ....

3 Triangle A has coordinates (-1,1), (-3,1) and (-3,3).
    a) Using appropriate axes draw triangle A.
    b) Enlarge triangle A by **i)** scale factor -3, centre (0,0). Label this triangle B. **ii)** scale factor -$\frac{1}{2}$, centre (0,1). Label this triangle C.
    c) i) Describe fully the transformation that maps triangle B onto triangle A.
       ii) Describe fully the transformation that maps triangle C onto triangle A.

Transformations

1 **The grid shows three triangles A, B and C.**

   a) Describe fully a single transformation that would

      map triangle A onto…

      i) triangle B ....

      ii) triangle C ....

   b) Describe fully a single transformation that would

      map triangle B onto triangle C.

      ....

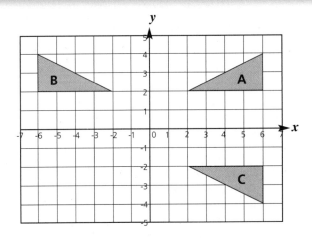

2 **The grid shows three quadrilaterals A, B and C.**

   a) Describe fully a single transformation that would

      map quadrilateral A onto…

      i) quadrilateral B ....

      ii) quadrilateral C ....

   b) Describe fully a single transformation that would

      map quadrilateral B onto quadrilateral C.

      ....

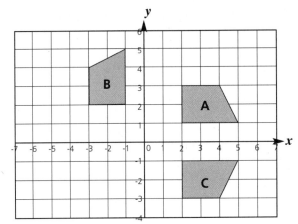

3 **The grid shows triangle A.**

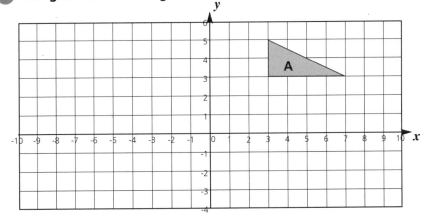

   a) Triangle A is reflected in the line

      $x = 1$. Draw and label this triangle B.

   b) Triangle A is reflected in the line

      $y = 1$. Draw and label this triangle C.

   c) Describe fully the single

      transformation that would map

      triangle B onto triangle C.

      ....

      ....

4   **a)** Quadrilateral A has coordinates (3,3), (6,3), (7,6) and (5,6). On a suitable grid draw quadrilateral A.

     b) Quadrilateral A is reflected in the line $x = 2$. Draw and label this quadrilateral B.

     c) Quadrilateral A is reflected in the line $y = 0$. Draw and label this quadrilateral C.

     d) Quadrilateral A is rotated 270° clockwise about the origin (0,0). Draw and label this quadrilateral D.

     e) Describe fully the single transformation that would map quadrilateral B onto quadrilateral C.

     f) Describe fully the single transformation that would map quadrilateral D onto quadrilateral C.

Vectors

1 **The diagram below shows eight different vectors.**

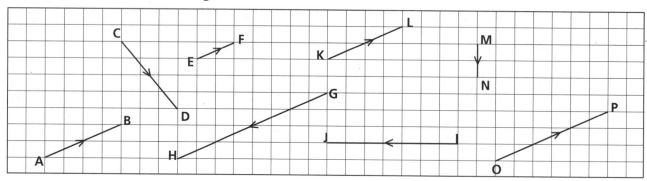

a) Write all the vectors in the diagram in the form $\begin{pmatrix} x \\ y \end{pmatrix}$.

$\overrightarrow{AB} = \begin{pmatrix} \ \\ \ \end{pmatrix}$, $\overrightarrow{CD} = \begin{pmatrix} \ \\ \ \end{pmatrix}$, $\overrightarrow{EF} = \begin{pmatrix} \ \\ \ \end{pmatrix}$, $\overrightarrow{GH} = \begin{pmatrix} \ \\ \ \end{pmatrix}$ $\overrightarrow{IJ} = \begin{pmatrix} \ \\ \ \end{pmatrix}$ $\overrightarrow{KL} = \begin{pmatrix} \ \\ \ \end{pmatrix}$, $\overrightarrow{MN} = \begin{pmatrix} \ \\ \ \end{pmatrix}$, $\overrightarrow{OP} = \begin{pmatrix} \ \\ \ \end{pmatrix}$

b) What is the relationship between the following vectors?

i) $\overrightarrow{AB}$ and $\overrightarrow{KL}$ ....

ii) $\overrightarrow{AB}$ and $\overrightarrow{EF}$ ....

iii) $\overrightarrow{AB}$ and $\overrightarrow{GH}$ ....

iv) $\overrightarrow{AB}$ and $\overrightarrow{OP}$ ....

c) Complete the following using the vectors in part **a)**. Give your answers in the form $\begin{pmatrix} x \\ y \end{pmatrix}$.

i) $\overrightarrow{AB} + \overrightarrow{CD}$ ....

ii) $\overrightarrow{AB} - \overrightarrow{CD}$ ....

iii) $\overrightarrow{HG} + \overrightarrow{EF}$ ....

iv) $\overrightarrow{HG} - \overrightarrow{GH}$ ....

v) $\overrightarrow{IJ} + \overrightarrow{OP}$ ....

vi) $2\overrightarrow{KL} + \overrightarrow{GH}$ ....

vii) $\overrightarrow{IJ} + \overrightarrow{MN}$ ....

viii) $\frac{1}{2} \overrightarrow{GH} - \overrightarrow{KL}$ ....

ix) $\overrightarrow{OP} - \overrightarrow{PO}$ ....

x) $\overrightarrow{AB} + \overrightarrow{CD} + \overrightarrow{MN}$ ....

2 If a = $\begin{pmatrix} 3 \\ 4 \end{pmatrix}$, b = $\begin{pmatrix} 2 \\ 3 \end{pmatrix}$, c = $\begin{pmatrix} -4 \\ -3 \end{pmatrix}$ and d = $\begin{pmatrix} 4 \\ -1 \end{pmatrix}$, on a suitable grid draw diagrams to represent...

   a) 2a **b)** 2c **c)** a + b **d)** a + c **e)** b + c **f)** b – c **g)** c – d **h)** c + 2d

3 **a)** Which vector is in the same direction as $\begin{pmatrix} 6 \\ -3 \end{pmatrix}$ but is twice as long?

   b) Which vector is in the opposite direction as $\begin{pmatrix} 6 \\ -3 \end{pmatrix}$ but is one third as long?

Vectors Proofs and 3-D Coordinates

1 OAB is a triangle. P is the midpoint of OA. $\overrightarrow{OA}$ = a and $\overrightarrow{OB}$ = b.

Express the following vectors in terms of a and/or b:

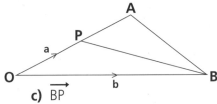

a) $\overrightarrow{AB}$

b) $\overrightarrow{PA}$

c) $\overrightarrow{BP}$

....

....

2 OABC is a rectangle. P and Q are the midpoints of AB and OC respectively. $\overrightarrow{OA}$ = a and $\overrightarrow{OC}$ = c.

a) Express the following vectors in terms of **a** and/or **c**.

    i) $\overrightarrow{CB}$ ....

    ii) $\overrightarrow{AB}$ ....

    iii) $\overrightarrow{PB}$ ....

    iv) $\overrightarrow{OQ}$ ....

    v) $\overrightarrow{PC}$ ....

    vi) $\overrightarrow{AQ}$ ....

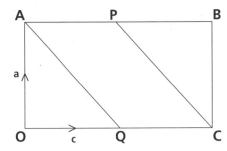

b) What can you deduce about shape APCQ? Explain your answer.

....

....

3 OABC is a parallelogram. P is a point on OA so that OP = $\frac{1}{3}$ OA. Q is a point on OC so that OQ = $\frac{1}{3}$

OC. X is a point on AB so that AX = $\frac{1}{3}$ AB. Y is a point on CB so that CY = $\frac{1}{3}$ CB.

$\overrightarrow{OA}$ = a and $\overrightarrow{OA}$ = c.

a) Express the following vectors in terms of **a** and/or **c**:

    i) $\overrightarrow{OP}$ ....

    ii) $\overrightarrow{OQ}$ ....

    iii) $\overrightarrow{PQ}$ ....

    iv) $\overrightarrow{BX}$ ....

    v) $\overrightarrow{BY}$ ....

    vi) $\overrightarrow{XY}$ ....

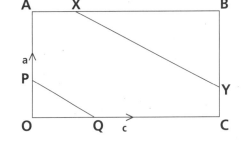

b) What can you deduce about shape PXYQ? Explain your answer.

....

....

4 P, Q, R and S are the midpoints of sides AB, BC, CD and DA of parallelogram ABCD respectively. Prove that PQRS is also a parallelogram.

5 G and H are the midpoints of sides AB and AC of triangle ABC respectively.
    a) Prove that triangle AGH and ABC are similar.
    b) What is the ratio of the two triangles' areas?

6 Draw axes from -5 to 5 on the x-axis and -3 to 4 on the y-axis.
    a) Draw and label A (4,2), B (-5,2), C (-4,-2)
    b) Draw and label a fourth coordinate D to produce a parallelogram ABCD.

7 The four base coordinates of a cube are (0,0,0), (3,0,0), (3,3,0) and (0,3,0).
    Draw a 3-D graph and write down the other four coordinates.

Constructions

1 **a)** Construct a triangle ABC with sides AB = 4cm, BC = 3cm and angle ABC = 40°.

b) On your triangle ABC from part **a)**, construct the bisector of angle BAC.

2 **a)** Construct a triangle PQR where PQ is 6cm, QR is 5cm and PR is 2cm.

b) Construct the perpendicular bisector of PQ. Where this line meets QR, label it S.

3 The sketch opposite shows three towns A, B and C. B is on a bearing of 040° from A. C is due East of A, and B is on a bearing of 300° from C. C is 40km from A. Construct an accurate scale drawing.

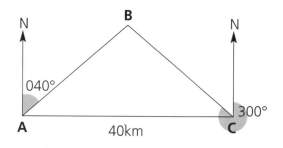

4 Showing all construction lines, and by using a pair of compasses and a ruler, construct the perpendicular bisector of each side of this equilateral triangle.

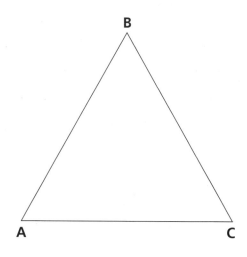

Constructions

5 **Using the line AB below as a starting point, use a pair of compasses and a ruler to do the following.**

a) Construct a 90° angle at A.

b) Construct a 90° angle at B.

c) Complete the construction to make a square. (You must show all of your construction lines.)

A _____ B

6 **In the space below draw a triangle XYZ.**

a) Construct the bisectors of the three angles $\hat{X}$, $\hat{Y}$ and $\hat{Z}$. You must show all of your construction lines.

b) What do you notice? ....

7 Using only a ruler and a pair of compasses, construct the following.
a) An equilateral triangle of side 3cm
b) A square of side 6cm.

8 Construct the following triangles using a ruler and a pair of compasses.
a)   **b)**   **c)**   **d)**

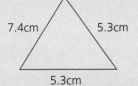
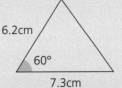
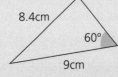
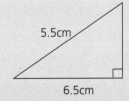

Loci

1 The points B, C and D represent three schools Biggley, Chiggley and Diggley. Pupils are entitled to a free bus pass if they live within 5km of the school they attend. Some pupils would be entitled to a free bus pass to all three schools. Draw an accurate diagram to show the region in which these pupils live.

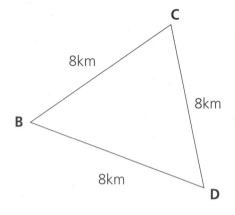

2 A goat is tethered by a rope 4m long to a rail PQ 8m long. The rope can move along the rail from P to Q. Draw an accurate diagram of the locus of points showing the area where the goat can eat grass.

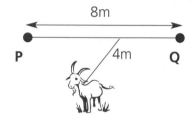

3 Draw a triangle ABC where AB = 7cm, BC = 9cm and AB̂C = 90°.
  a) Draw the locus of points inside the triangle that are equidistant from A and B.
  b) Draw the locus of points inside the triangle that are equidistant from B and C.
  c) Find and label a point D that is equidistant from A and B and equidistant from B and C.

4 Draw the same triangle ABC as for question 3.
  a) Draw the locus of points equidistant from line AB and AC.
  b) A point (P) moves inside triangle ABC, equidistant from AB and AC and greater than 6cm away from C. Show the locus of points where P can move.

Perimeter

1 Calculate the perimeter of the following shapes. Where lengths are not given, use a ruler to measure the sides.

a)

6.2cm

2.6cm

1.7cm

2.8cm

....

....

b)

2.5cm

4.2cm

7.1cm

3.3cm

0.7cm   4.3cm

....

....

c)

....

....

d)

....

....

e)

....

....

f)

....

....

Perimeter, Circumference and Arcs

2 A window is in the shape of a semi-circle on top of a rectangle, as shown in the diagram.

AB = 1.8m and BC = 90cm. Calculate the perimeter of the window to 3 sig. fig. π = 3.14

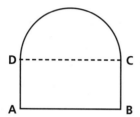

....

....

....

....

3 Mrs Jones' garden is rectangular. At each end there is a semi-circular flower bed and the rest of the garden is lawn, as shown in the diagram. If AB = 10m and BC = 8m, calculate the perimeter of the lawn.

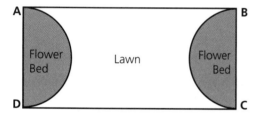

....

....

....

....

4 Christmas decorations are made using the template shown.
Ribbon is sewn around the outside edge of each decoration.
How much ribbon is needed to make 15 decorations? π = 3.14

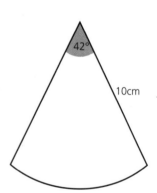

....

....

....

5 The minor sector OXY is cut out of a circle and discarded. The
two radii OX and OY are then joined edge to edge to form a
cone as shown opposite. Calculate the radius of the base of
the cone (to 1.d.p).

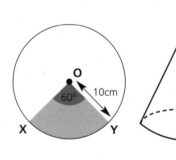

....

....

....

6 Calculate the circumference of the following circles to 1 decimal place. Take π = 3.14
   a) Radius = 12cm **b)** Radius = 1.2cm **c)** Diameter = 12cm **d)** Diameter = 120cm

7 Sector OAB (shaded) is cut out of a circle with a radius of 16cm.
   a) Calculate the perimeter of sector OAB (to 3 s.f.).
   b) Calculate the perimeter of the major sector left over (to 1 d.p.).

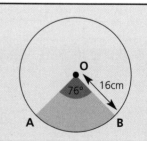

1 Estimate the area of the following shapes. Each square has an area of **1cm².**

a)

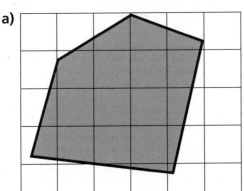

b)

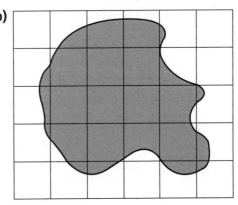

....

2 Calculate the area of the following shapes. They are not drawn to scale.

a)

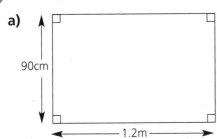

90cm

1.2m

b)

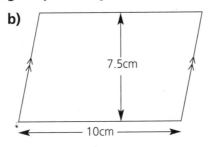

7.5cm

10cm

c)

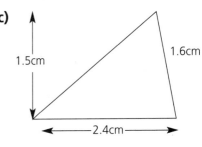

1.5cm

1.6cm

2.4cm

....
....

d)

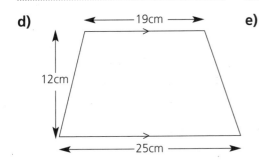

19cm

12cm

25cm

e)

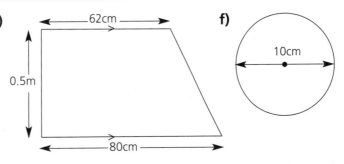

62cm

0.5m

80cm

f)

10cm

....
....

3 Calculate the shaded area of the following shapes. They are not drawn to scale. Take π = **3.14**

a)

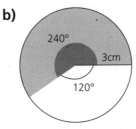

40°
5cm

b)

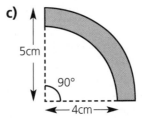

240°
3cm
120°

c)

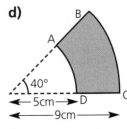

5cm
90°
4cm

d)

B
A
40°
5cm D C
9cm

....
....

Area of Quadrilaterals, Triangles and Circles

4 A circular table has an area of 11.304m². Calculate its radius to 1 d.p.

....
....
....

5 A circular flower bed has an area of 7.065m². Calculate its radius to 1 d.p.

....
....
....

6 Calculate the area of the following shapes, rounding to 1 d.p. where necessary. They are not drawn to scale.

a)

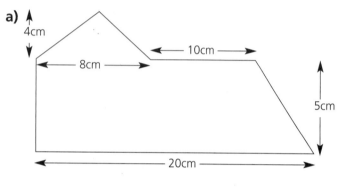

b)

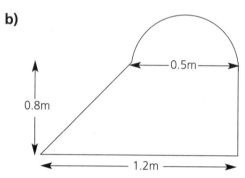

....
....
....

....
....
....

7 Find the shaded area when...

a) r = 6cm, ? = 70°

....

b) r = 14cm, ? = 104°

....

c) r = 5cm, ? = 80°

....

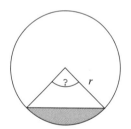

8 Find ? and hence the shaded area when...

a) AB = 10cm, r = 10cm

....

b) AB = 8cm, r = 5cm

....

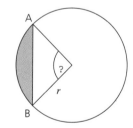

9 A property developer decides to varnish the floorboards in the living room of one of his houses. A plan of the floor is shown here.
It is not to scale. One tin of varnish will cover 16m² and costs £4.99.
If he wants to apply two coats of varnish to the whole floor, how much will it cost him?

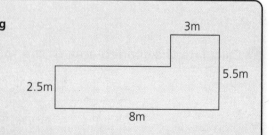

10 Find the radius of the circle...
a) when ? = 90°, A = 20cm²
b) when ? = 30°, A = 35cm²
c) when ? = 150°, A = 114cm²

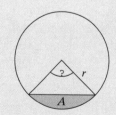

1 Calculate the surface area of the following solids, rounding to 3 s.f. where necessary.

a)

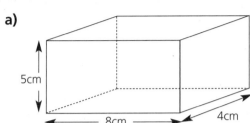

5cm

8cm   4cm

b)

2.8cm

3.2cm   10cm

....

....

....

....

....

....

2 A cylindrical drum has a radius of 5cm and a height of 12cm. Find the total surface area of the drum including both ends to 3 s.f.

....

....

....

3 A child's night light is spherical in shape, with radius 4cm. Calculate the surface area of the light to 3 s.f.

....

....

4 Calculate the total surface area of the cone-shaped tent opposite, including the base. Give your answer in terms of π.

....

....

5m

6m

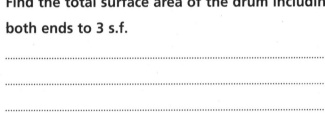

5 Calculate the surface area of a sphere with...
a) radius 7cm b) radius 3.7cm c) diameter 10cm d) diameter 28cm.

6 Calculate the surface area of the shape shown opposite, which is half a sphere on top of a cone. Give your answer in terms of π.

3cm

6cm

Volume

1 **Calculate the volume of the following solids.**

a)

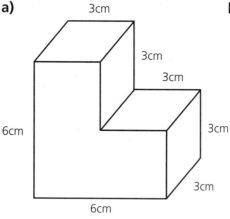

3cm

3cm

3cm

6cm

3cm

3cm

6cm

b)

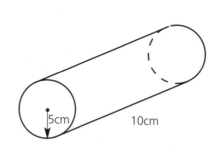

5cm

10cm

c)

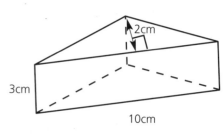

2cm

3cm

10cm

....

....

....

....

....

....

....

....

....

2 **a)** The following cylinder has a volume of 314cm³.

Calculate the missing length represented by x

($\pi = 3.14$).

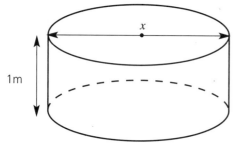

x

1m

b) The following solid has a volume of 100cm³.

Calculate the missing length represented by x.

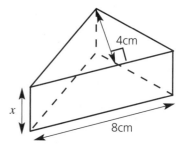

4cm

x

8cm

....

....

....

....

....

....

3 **A globe has a diameter of 30cm.**

Calculate its volume to 3 s.f.

....

....

....

....

....

....

Volume

4 A firework has a conical shape with a base radius of 2cm and a height of 7.5cm. Calculate its volume.

....

....

....

....

....

....

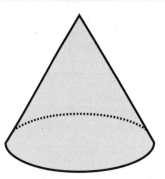

5 The tank opposite contains water. The depth of the water is 50cm. All the water is poured into a cylindrical tank that has a diameter of 44cm. Calculate the depth of the water in the cylindrical tank to 1 d.p. (π = 3.14).

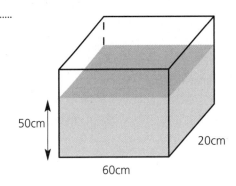

....

....

....

....

6 A cuboid measuring 12cm x 15cm x 20cm has the same surface area as a sphere of radius *r* cm. Calculate *r* correct to 3 s.f.

....

....

....

7 A sector is cut from a round piece of cheese. Calculate the volume of the piece of cheese.

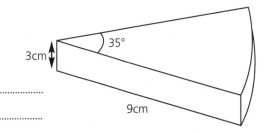

....

....

....

8 A cylindrical mug has internal radius 5cm and internal height 8cm.
a) Calculate the volume of liquid it can hold to 3 s.f. (π = 3.14)
b) If 500cm³ of liquid is poured into the mug, what would the depth of liquid be in the mug?

9 Find the length of each edge of a cube that has the same volume as a sphere of radius 8cm. Give your answer to 3 s.f.

Maps and Scale Drawings

1 a) Draw an accurate scale drawing of this garden, using a scale of 1cm to represent 2.5m.

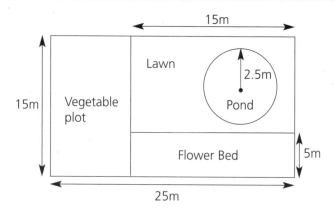

b) What is the actual diagonal distance across the garden in metres?

....

2 This is part of a map of Devon and Cornwall drawn to a scale of 1cm : 10km.

a) What is the direct distance from Launceston to Exeter?

....

....

b) What is the direct distance between Bodmin and Looe?

....

....

c) Name two places that are a direct distance of 43km from Tavistock.

....

....

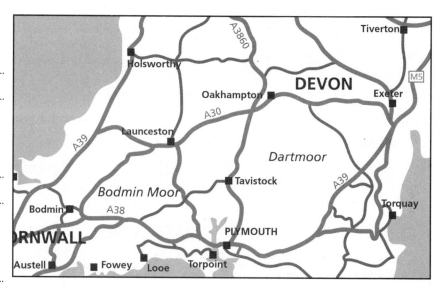

3 a) Draw an accurate scale drawing of a rectangular field 80m long and 50m wide. **b)** By measurement, find the actual distance diagonally from one corner to the opposite corner, to the nearest metre.

4 The diagram opposite shows a sketch of one side of a house.
a) Draw an accurate scale drawing using a scale of 1cm to 1m.
b) By measurement, find the actual height of the house (*x*).

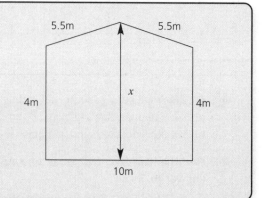

Effects of Enlargement

1 Two figures are similar. The ratio of two corresponding lengths is 2 : 3.

    a) What is the ratio of their areas? ....

    b) What is the ratio of their volumes? ....

2 Two figures are similar. The ratio of their areas is 6.25 : 16. What is the ratio of their volumes?

....

....

3 The diagram shows two similar figures.
The height of Figure A is 12cm and the
height of Figure B is 27cm.

Figure B

Figure A

12cm

27cm

    a) If the surface area of Figure A is 72cm²,
        calculate the surface area of Figure B.

    b) If the volume of Figure B is 243cm³,
        calculate the volume of Figure A.

    ....

    ....

    ....

4 Two figures are similar. The volume of Figure A is 108cm³ and the volume of Figure B is 500cm³.
If the surface area of Figure B is 60cm², what is the surface area of Figure A?

....

....

....

5 Two figures are similar. The surface area of Figure A is 150cm² and the surface area of
Figure B is 294cm². If the volume of Figure A is 275cm³, what is the volume of Figure B?

....

....

....

6 Three bottles are similar. Bottle A has a height of 6cm, a surface area of 12cm² and a volume of 9cm³.
    a) If Bottle B has a surface area of 75cm² calculate: **i)** its height **ii)** its volume.
    b) If Bottle C has a volume of 72cm³ calculate: **i)** its height **ii)** its surface area.

7 Is it possible for Figure A, which has a height of 22cm and a volume of 135cm³, to be similar to Figure B, which
has a height of 33cm and a volume of 320cm³? Explain your answer.

Converting Measurements

1 **Convert...**

a) 450cm into metres

....

....

b) 3.5 litres into millilitres

....

....

c) 1.25kg into grams

....

....

d) 6874g into kg

....

....

e) 45km into metres

....

....

f) 0.55cm into mm

....

....

2 **Convert these lengths into metres.**

a) 1005cm

....

....

b) 1.937km

....

....

c) 2650mm

....

....

3 **Put these weights into order of size, smallest first.**

420g   4kg   39.5kg   4220mg   0.405kg

....

....

4 **Convert...**

a) 45cm into inches

....

....

b) 6 ounces into grams

....

....

c) 5 gallons into litres

....

....

5 **Terry is 1.5m tall. Jake is 68 inches tall. Who is taller and by how much?**

....

....

....

6 **Put these lengths into decreasing order of size:**

1km   900m   1200m   11 000cm   1050 000mm

7 **Convert...**

a) 3 miles into km **b)** 12km into miles **c)** 4.5 pounds into grams **d)** 360g into pounds **e)** 12 pints into litres
f) 22.5 litres into pints

8 **Sue ran a 10km race. How many yards did she run altogether? (1760 yards = 1 mile)**

9 **Write in cm²**
a) 460mm² **b)** 0.76m²

10 **Write in cm³**
a) 500mm³ **b)** 0.03m³

Bearings

1 The diagram shows the position of the coastguard (C), the beach (B) and a yacht (Y).

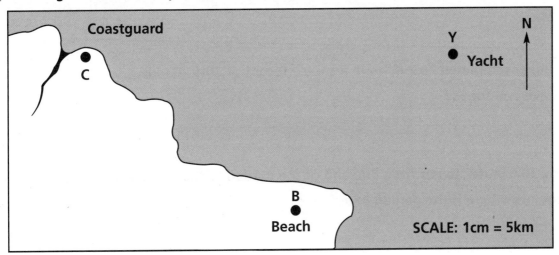

a) What is the bearing of the following?

   i) Y from C ....

   iii) B from C ....

   v) C from Y ....

   ii) Y from B ....

   iv) B from Y ....

   vi) C from B ....

b) What is the actual distance from the following?

   i) C to B ....

   ii) C to Y ....

   iii) B to Y ....

2 The map shows the position of four towns A, B, C and D on an island. A helicopter flies directly from A to B, then B to C, then C to D and finally D back to A. On what four bearings must it fly?

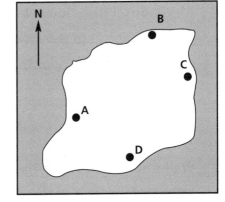

A ➤ B ....

B ➤ C ....

C ➤ D ....

D ➤ A ....

3 What is the back-bearing for the following bearings?
  a) 058° **b)** 190° **c)** 306°

4 An explorer walks 1000m on a bearing of 070° and then walks 2000m on a bearing of 160°.
  a) Draw an accurate scale drawing of his route.
  b) By measurement, find the bearing he must follow to return directly to his starting point.

5 Treasure is buried on an island according to the following instructions: "The treasure lies on a bearing of 100° from the coconut tree and on a bearing of 200° from the cactus plant. The cactus plant is 20m due east of the coconut tree." Draw a scale drawing using 1cm to 5m to show the position of the treasure.

6 B lies on a bearing of 080° from A and AB = 12km.
  C lies on a bearing of 280° from A and AC = 15km.
  Use the cosine rule to find the direct distance, BC (to 1 d.p.).

Compound Measures

1 Work out the time taken to travel 92km at an average speed of 55km/h.

....

2 A marathon runner completed 26.2 miles in a course record of 2hrs 20mins.
What was his average speed?

....

3 A tortoise took 20 minutes to get from one end of the garden to the other. His average speed is
2cm per second. How long is the garden in metres?

....

....

4 A boat travels for $2\frac{1}{2}$ hours at 100km/h and then for $1\frac{1}{2}$ hours at 80km/h. Calculate its average
speed for the whole journey.

....

....

5 A cylindrical tree stump weighs 15kg.
Its dimensions are shown opposite.
Calculate the density of the wood (to 1 d.p.).

....

....

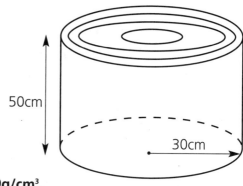

50cm

30cm

6 Water has a density of 1g/cm³ and ice has a density of 0.9g/cm³.
450cm³ of water is frozen. By how much does the volume of the water change when it freezes?

....

....

....

7 **a)** Change 30 metres per second into km per hour.
b) A car travels 30 metres per second for $3\frac{1}{2}$ hours. How far does it travel in km?

8 **The density of oak wood is 800kg per m³.**
a) Change this to g per cm³.
b) How much does a solid oak table top measuring 110cm by 80cm by 5cm weigh?

Probability

1 Tim has ten cards (shown below). They are placed face down and mixed up.

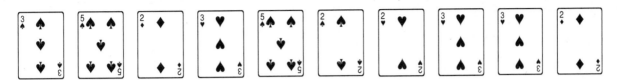

a) What is the probability that a card picked at random will be the following?

   i) a 2 .... **ii)** a 3 .... **iii)** a 4 ....

   iv) a 5 .... **v)** not a 2 .... **vi)** not a 3 ....

b) Here is a probability scale:

```
                                   0.5
  0 |——+——+——+——+——+——+——+——+——+——| 1
```

On the scale above…

   i) mark with an A the probability that a card picked at random will be a 2

   ii) mark with a B the probability that a card picked at random will be a 3

   iii) mark with a C the probability that a card picked at random will be a 4

   iv) mark with a D the probability that a card picked at random will be a 5.

2 A bag contains 4 red counters, 5 blue counters and 9 yellow counters.
A counter is picked out at random. What is the probability that it is the following?

a) red .... **b)** not red .... **c)** blue ....

d) not blue .... **e)** yellow .... **f)** not yellow ....

3 A page in a calendar shows the month of June.
If a date is chosen at random, what is the probability that it is the following?

a) an even number .... **b)** an odd number ....

c) a prime number .... **d)** a weekday ....

e) not a weekday ....

JUNE						
S	M	T	W	T	F	S
			1	2	3	4	5
6	7	8	9	10	11	12
13	14	15	16	17	18	19
20	21	22	23	24	25	26
27	28	29	30			

4 Jack has the following fair spinner. He spins it.

a) What is the probability that the spinner does not land on a 1?

....

b) What is the probability that the spinner does not land on a 2?

....

c) What is the probability that the spinner lands on a 3?

....

Probability

5 **Vicky has two sets of cards, A and B as shown below:**

a) Complete all the possible outcomes if two cards are picked, one from A and one from B, at random.

b) What is the probability that the two cards picked are **i)** both 2s? ....

   ii) both the same suit? .... **iii)** not the same suit? ....

6 **Brian's pencil case contains blue, black, red and green biros only. The probability of picking out a biro of a certain colour is shown in the table. What is the probability that the biro picked out is red?**

Colour of biro	Probability of picking that colour
Blue	0.2
Black	0.35
Red	....
Green	0.15

7 **On her way to work, Safia has to drive through heavy traffic. The probability that Safia will arrive at work on time is 0.4 and that she will arrive late is 0.25. What is the probability that she will arrive early?**

....

8 **A bag contains 8 blue marbles, 6 red marbles and 2 green marbles. One marble is pulled out at random and not put back into the bag. A second marble is then picked out at random.**

   a) What is the probability that the second marble picked out is blue, if the first marble picked out was green? ....

   b) What is the probability that the second marble picked out is green, if the first marble picked out was also green? ....

9 **A box contains 7 red balls and 3 blue balls. A ball is picked out at random.**
   What is the probability that it is **a)** red? **b)** not red? **c)** blue? **d)** not blue? **e)** red or blue? **f)** black?

10 **A kitchen cupboard contains tins of baked beans, peas, carrots and potatoes only. The probability of picking a tin of potatoes is $\frac{1}{12}$, while the probability of picking a tin of carrots is three times that of a tin of potatoes, and a tin of peas is twice that of a tin of carrots.**
   a) What is the probability of picking: **i)** a tin of carrots? **ii)** a tin of peas? **iii)** a tin of baked beans?
   b) What is the probability of not picking: **i)** a tin of carrots? **ii)** a tin of peas? **iii)** a tin of baked beans?
   c) If the cupboard contains 4 tins of baked beans, how many tins are there in the cupboard altogether?

Probability

1 Two fair dice are thrown and the two numbers are added together to give a total score.

a) Complete the sample space diagram below to show all the scores.

<table>
<thead>
<tr><th colspan="7">First Dice</th></tr>
<tr><th>+</th><th>1</th><th>2</th><th>3</th><th>4</th><th>5</th><th>6</th></tr>
</thead>
<tbody>
<tr><td>1</td><td>2</td><td>3</td><td>4</td><td></td><td></td><td></td></tr>
<tr><td>2</td><td>3</td><td>4</td><td></td><td></td><td></td><td></td></tr>
<tr><td>3</td><td>4</td><td></td><td></td><td></td><td></td><td></td></tr>
<tr><td>4</td><td></td><td></td><td></td><td></td><td></td><td></td></tr>
<tr><td>5</td><td></td><td></td><td></td><td></td><td></td><td></td></tr>
<tr><td>6</td><td></td><td></td><td></td><td></td><td></td><td></td></tr>
</tbody>
</table>

(left axis label: Second Dice)

b) What is the probability that the total score will be…

i) equal to 7? ....

ii) greater than 7? ....

iii) a prime number? ....

iv) a square number? ....

v) greater than 12? ....

vi) a multiple of 3? ....

vii) a factor of 12? ....

2 Francis and Jim have the following coins in their pockets:

Francis	Jim

Two coins are picked out at random, one from Francis' pocket and one from Jim's pocket. The values of the two coins are added together.

a) Complete the sample space diagram below to show all the values.

<table>
<thead>
<tr><th colspan="6">Francis' Coin</th></tr>
</thead>
<tbody>
<tr><td></td><td></td><td></td><td></td><td></td><td></td></tr>
<tr><td></td><td></td><td></td><td></td><td></td><td></td></tr>
<tr><td></td><td></td><td></td><td></td><td></td><td></td></tr>
<tr><td></td><td></td><td></td><td></td><td></td><td></td></tr>
<tr><td></td><td></td><td></td><td></td><td></td><td></td></tr>
<tr><td></td><td></td><td></td><td></td><td></td><td></td></tr>
</tbody>
</table>

(left axis label: Jim's Coin)

b) What is the probability that the total value of the two coins added together is the following?

i) equal to 6p ....

ii) equal to 11p ....

iii) less than 10p ....

iv) greater than 40p ....

v) less than 40p ....

vi) equal to 40p ....

3 Bruce has an ordinary fair dice. Robin has the fair spinner shown opposite.
The spinner is spun and the dice is thrown to give two numbers.
a) Draw a sample space diagram to show all the possible scores if the numbers are multiplied together.
b) What is the probability that the score is **i)** equal to 12? **ii)** equal to 24? **iii)** a multiple of 10?
  iv) a factor of 4? **v)** an odd number? **vi)** an even number?

Probability

1 There are a number of red, white and blue beads in a bag. The probability of picking a red bead is $\frac{1}{3}$ and the probability of picking a blue bead is $\frac{1}{5}$.

a) What is the probability of picking a red or blue bead?

....

b) What is the probability of picking a white or red bead?

....

2 There are 52 cards in a pack. One is picked at random. What is the probability that it is...

a) a heart or a diamond? ....

b) a heart or a king? ....

3 If two fair dice are thrown, what is the probability of the results being...

a) two sixes? ....

b) two odd numbers? ....

4 There are 10 discs in a bag, of which 3 are blue. Two discs are picked out at random without being replaced. What is the probability of getting two blue discs?

....

5 Vicky has a set of five cards, shown below. They are placed face down. She also has an ordinary fair dice.

A card is picked at random and the dice is thrown.

a) What is the probability of throwing a 3 or 4 with the dice and picking a card with a 2 on it?

....

b) What is the probability of throwing an odd number with the dice and picking a card with an odd number on it?

....

6 A box contains 3 blue, 4 yellow, 5 red and 2 green sweets. One sweet is taken out and eaten. A second is then taken out. What is the probability that...
a) both sweets are green?
b) both sweets are the same colour?

Probability

1 **The probability that Steve arrives at school on time on any particular day is 0.7**

a) Complete the tree diagram for two school days, Monday and Tuesday.

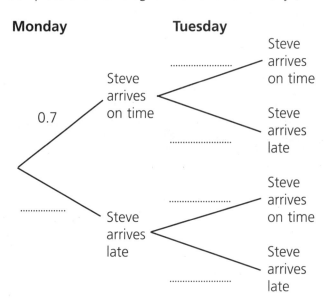

Monday **Tuesday**

.... Steve arrives on time

Steve arrives on time

0.7

.... Steve arrives late

....

Steve arrives late

.... Steve arrives on time

.... Steve arrives late

b) What is the probability that…

i) Steve arrives on time on Monday and Tuesday?

....

ii) Steve arrives late on Monday and Tuesday?

....

iii) Steve arrives late on Monday only?

....

iv) Steve arrives late on Tuesday only?

....

v) Steve arrives late on one day only?

....

2 **Vicky, Donna and Petra are going to have two races. The probability that Vicky wins either of the two races is 0.5, while the probability that Donna wins either of the two races is 0.3**

a) What is the probability of Petra winning either of the two races? ....

b) Complete the tree diagram.

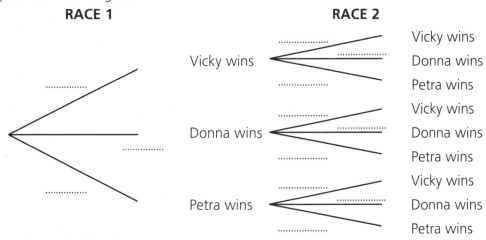

RACE 1 **RACE 2**

.... Vicky wins

Vicky wins .... Donna wins

.... Petra wins

.... Vicky wins

Donna wins .... Donna wins

.... Petra wins

.... Vicky wins

Petra wins .... Donna wins

.... Petra wins

c) What is the probability that…

i) Vicky wins both races?... **ii)** Vicky does not win a race? ....

iii) Donna wins Race 1 and Petra wins Race 2? ....

iv) Race 1 and Race 2 are won by different girls? ....

3 **The probability that Julie does her school homework on any particular day is 0.8.**
a) Draw a tree diagram to show all the probabilities for two days.
b) Using the tree diagram, what is the probability that Julie **i)** does her homework on both days **ii)** does her homework on one day only **iii)** does not do her homework on either day?

Probability

1 **The following fair spinner is spun 120 times.**

a) How many times would you expect the

spinner to land on…

i) a 1? ………………………………… **ii)** a 2? ………………………………… **iii)** a 3? …………………………………

b) The actual number of times the spinner landed on a 1, 2 and 3 is shown in the table below.

For each number, calculate the relative frequency.

Number	Number of Times Landed	Relative Frequency
1	66	**i)** ………………………………………
2	38	**ii)** ………………………………………
3	16	**iii)** ………………………………………

2 **Jane flips a coin 50, 100, 150, 200 and 250 times. She records the number of tails she gets in a table (shown opposite):**

Number of Flips	Number of Tails	Relative Frequency
50	20	0.4
100	44	**i)** ……………………
150	80	**ii)** ……………………
200	92	**iii)** ……………………
250	120	**iv)** ……………………

a) Complete the table by calculating the missing relative frequencies.

b) On the grid below draw a bar graph to show the relative frequency of the coin landing on tails.

c) If Jane kept flipping the coin, what would you expect the relative frequency of the coin landing on tails to become? Explain why.

………………………………………………

………………………………………………

………………………………………………

………………………………………………

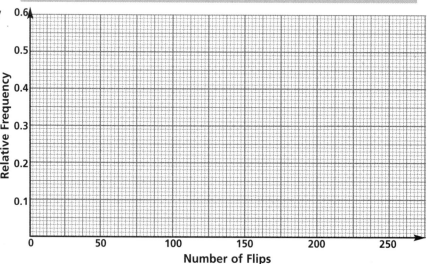

3 **Below are the results of an experiment where a dice was thrown and the number of sixes was recorded.**

Number of Throws	30	60	90	120	150	180	210	240	270	300	330	360
Number of Sixes Thrown	3	5	10	16	23	28	35	42	47	49	52	59
Relative Frequency												

a) Complete the table by calculating the missing relative frequencies.

b) Draw a bar graph to show the relative frequency of throwing a 6.

c) How many sixes would you expect to be thrown if the experiment was continued and the dice was thrown 1500 times?

Problem Solving and Handling Data

1 Fill in the empty boxes in this flow chart to complete the data handling cycle.

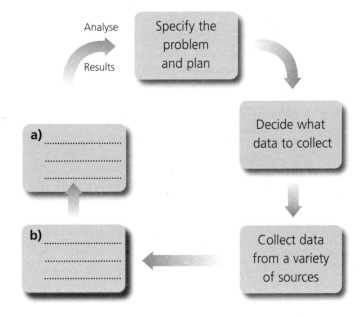

2 Give three examples of possible sources of data. Describe each one as primary or secondary.

a) ....

b) ....

c) ....

3 You are asked to conduct research into the amount of exercise that your classmates take outside of school. Using the data handling cycle, explain what processes you will go through in order to observe, collect and make a conclusion from your research. Suggest some possible ways in which the research might be developed further.

....

....

....

....

....

....

4 Suggest another problem for which you could use the data handling cycle.

....

....

....

Collecting Data

1 **What is the difference between primary data and secondary data?**

....

....

2 **a)** What is sampling? ....

b) What is the difference between a random sample and a stratified sample?

....

....

c) A recent survey carried out in Manchester suggests that 90% of the national population prefer football to rugby. The survey was conducted on 200 males. Has this survey provided reliable data? Explain why.

....

....

3 The table shows the gender and number of students in each year group. Mark is carrying out a survey about how much pocket money students are given. He decides to take a stratified sample of 150 students from the whole school.

Year Group	No. of Boys	No. of Girls	Total
7	160	120	280
8	108	132	240
9	158	117	275
10	85	70	155
11	140	110	250

a) Calculate how many in the stratified sample should be:

i) students from year 8 ....

ii) girls from year 11 ....

b) i) Which year group should have 35 pupils in the sample? ....

ii) How many of these 35 should be boys / girls?

....

4 Jenny is concerned about the breakfast habits of the pupils at her school. She decides to use a questionnaire to find out what pupils have to eat for breakfast. She has chosen eight questions for her questionnaire. Decide whether each question is suitable or not suitable, giving a reason for your answer.

a) Everybody should eat breakfast. Don't you agree? ....

b) Do you eat breakfast? ....

c) What time do you get up in the morning? ....

d) Are you a vegetarian? ....

e) What year are you in? ....

f) What do you have to eat if you have breakfast? ....

g) If you eat breakfast do you have cereal, toast or other? ....

h) Do you brush your teeth before breakfast? ....

Collecting Data

5 Joe works in a supermarket. He decides to use a questionnaire to find out about the shopping habits of the customers who come into the store. Here is the first question:

'How old are you?' Tick the correct box.

Under 10 years		11 years to 20 years		21 years to 40 years		41 years to 60 years		61 years to 80 years		Over 80 years	

a) Make up two more suitable questions Joe could use for his questionnaire.

i) ....

ii) ....

b) Make up two questions that would not be suitable for his questionnaire.

i) ....

ii) ....

6 In a survey a group of pupils were asked, 'How long did you spend watching TV over the weekend?'

a) Design a suitable observation sheet to collect this information.

b) How would you make sure that the information obtained was from a random sample?

....

....

7 The table shows the number of employees in 5 different locations of a firm. A stratified sample is required for a survey. How many people should be chosen for each location?

....

....

Location	Employees
A	398
B	1011
C	409
D	207
E	1985

8 Molly works in a pizza parlour. She decides to use a questionnaire to find out about the eating habits of the people who come into the parlour.
a) Make up three suitable questions Molly could use for her questionnaire.
b) Make up three questions that are not suitable for her questionnaire.

9 Jimmy is carrying out a survey to investigate what the pupils in his school spend their pocket money on.
a) Design a suitable observation sheet for him to collect the information.
b) How could Jimmy make sure that the information collected was random?

Sorting Data

1 **What is the difference between discrete and continuous data?**

.... © Lonsdale

....

....

2 Jane is carrying out a traffic survey. She records the number of cars that pass her house every 30 seconds for a period of 20 minutes. Group her data by completing the frequency table below.

Number of cars

4 3 4 ~~1~~ 2 5 5 4 3 2
4 5 3 2 4 4 4 5 5 ~~1~~
2 4 3 5 4 3 3 5 2 4
2 4 3 5 2 ~~1~~ ~~1~~ 4 5 3

Number of Cars	Tally	Frequency
1	IIII	4
2		
3		
4		
5		

3 A survey was carried out on the number of residents in each house on a street. The results are given below:

4, 5, 3, 4, 3, 6, 1, 5, 4, 2, 3, 4, 5, 2, 4, 5, 5, 3, 4, 6
4, 2, 5, 3, 5, 2, 4, 3, 4, 1, 3, 4, 4, 1, 5, 2, 4, 5, 3, 4

a) In the space below group together the results in a frequency table.

b) What percentage of the houses have three or more residents? ....

4 The test results for a group of students are given below.

Group the data to complete the frequency table below.

31	61	40	63	65
78	52	57	~~15~~	35
77	~~11~~	68	46	68
64	70	26	87	49

Test Mark	Tally	Frequency
0–19	II	2
20–39		
40–59		
60–79		
80–99		

5 John recorded the temperature at midday every day for the month of June.

All the temperatures are to the nearest degree Celsius.

a) Group together John's results by completing the frequency table.

Temperature (°C)	Tally	Frequency
5 ≤ T < 10		
10 ≤ T < 15		
15 ≤ T < 20		
20 ≤ T < 25		

b) What percentage of the recorded midday temperatures in June are 15°C or more?

....

6 Bolton Wanderers scored the following number of goals in Premier League matches for the 2002/2003 season.
1, 1, 1, 1, 2, 1, 1, 0, 1, 1, 1, 1, 4, 1, 0, 1, 0, 1, 4
0, 0, 0, 1, 0, 1, 4, 1, 1, 0, 2, 1, 2, 0, 1, 0, 2, 0, 2
Group together the data in a frequency table.

7 Emma decided to measure the height (*h*) of all the students in her class.
Here are the results, to the nearest cm:
171, 178, 166, 173, 180, 173, 186, 176, 170, 184, 178, 174, 169, 189, 175, 182, 181, 171, 179, 164, 178, 175, 174,
191, 169, 178, 173, 188, 167, 192.
a) Sort the data into a frequency table using class intervals 160 ≤ *h* < 165, 165 ≤ *h* < 170, etc.
b) What percentage of the students in Emma's class have a height measurement of 170cm or more?

8 The individual weights of 40 people, to the nearest kg, are as follows:
79, 75, 68, 70, 83, 72, 81, 89, 61, 74, 80, 51, 84, 63, 73, 54, 76, 74, 80, 85, 94, 77, 71, 81, 70, 66, 87, 62, 59, 63, 63,
67, 75, 81, 80, 78, 60, 77, 61, 75.
Sort the data into a frequency table using appropriate class intervals.

Sorting Data

1 The following data shows the age (in years) of 30 shoppers in a supermarket.

41, 51, 8, 60, 21, 31, 41, 17, 68, 28, 34, 45, 46, 52, 74,

56, 10, 23, 47, 30, 34, 9, 42, 29, 55, 44, 38, 57, 47, 58

Using tens to form the 'stem' and units to form the 'leaves', draw a stem and leaf diagram to show the data.

2 A survey of 120 people was conducted to find out if they listen to the radio whilst driving. Complete the two way table to show the results.

	Men	Women	Total
Listen to Radio	32	....	73
Do Not Listen to Radio	....	24	....
Total	55	....	....

3 A survey of 200 Year 7, 8 and 9 pupils was carried out to find their favourite type of music from a choice of three: Pop, Rap or Dance.

a) Complete the two way table to show the results.

	Year 7	Year 8	Year 9	Total
Pop	42	....	18	....
Rap	....	12	....	41
Dance	14	....	31	69
Total	....	....	62	....

b) What percentage of the pupils chose Pop as their favourite type of music?

....

4 Here are the heights, to the nearest cm, of 30 students in a class:

171, 178, 166, 173, 180, 173, 186, 176, 170, 184, 178, 174, 169, 189, 175, 182, 181, 171, 179, 164, 178, 175, 174, 191, 169, 178, 173, 188, 167, 192

a) Using tens to form the 'stem' and units to form the 'leaves', draw a stem and leaf diagram to show the data.

b) What is the modal class of the data?

c) What is the median value of the data?

Averages and Spread

1 Janet carries out a survey on the number of passengers in cars that pass her house.

Here are the results:

Number of Passengers	Frequency	Frequency x No. of Passengers
0	11	
1	12	
2	6	
3	8	
4	3	

a) How many cars were there in her survey? ....

b) What is the modal number of passengers? ....

c) What is the median number of passengers? ....

d) What is the range of the number of passengers? ....

e) What is the mean number of passengers?

....

....

2 This graph shows the number of chocolate bars bought by pupils at a school tuck shop.

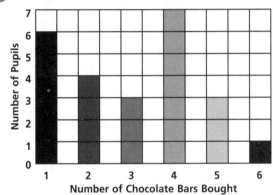

Number of Pupils / Number of Chocolate Bars Bought

a) How many pupils bought chocolate bars? ....

b) What is the modal number of bars bought? ....

c) What is the median number of bars bought? ....

d) What is the mean number of bars bought?

....

....

....

3 The table gives the recorded midday temperature every day for June.

a) Complete the table, including suitable headings for the last 2 columns.

Estimate the mean recorded temperature.

Temperature, T (°C)	Frequency	....	....
5 ≤ T < 10	3	7.5	3 × 7.5 = 22.5
10 ≤ T < 15	14	12.5	....
15 ≤ T < 20	11	....	....
20 ≤ T < 25	2		

b) In which class interval does the median lie? ....

c) What is the modal class? ....

4 During a PE lesson the boys have a 100m race. Their times were recorded and the results are shown below.

Time Taken, t (seconds)	12 < t ≤ 14	14 < t ≤ 16	16 < t ≤ 18	18 < t ≤ 20	20 < t ≤ 22	22 < t ≤ 24
Number of Boys	2	9	13	5	3	1

a) Calculate an estimate of the mean time. **b)** In which class interval does the median lie? **c)** Which class interval is the mode?

Displaying Data

1 **36 primary school children were asked to name their favourite pet. Draw a bar graph to show this information.**

$\frac{1}{3}$ said DOG

$\frac{1}{4}$ said CAT

$\frac{2}{9}$ said FISH

$\frac{1}{12}$ said RABBIT

... and the remainder said BIRD.

2 **In one week a travel agent sold 120 separate holidays. The table below shows the holiday destinations.**

Holiday Destination	No. of Holidays Sold
Spain	42
Greece	12
France	34
Cyprus	22
Italy	10

a) Draw and label a pie chart to represent these destinations.

b) What percentage of the holidays sold were for Spain?

....

c) What fraction of the holidays sold were for Greece?

....

3 **This bar chart shows the different types of milk sold in a supermarket and the actual number of pints sold on one day.**

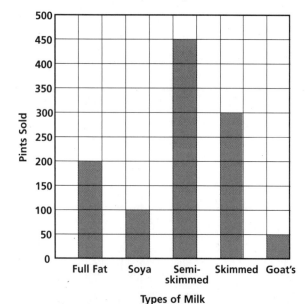

a) What was the second most popular type of milk sold? ....

b) How many pints of milk were sold in total?

....

c) In the space below draw a pictogram to show this data.

1 A group of factory workers were asked how long it took them to get to work.

This table shows the results. Construct a frequency diagram to show this information.

Time, t (minutes)	Number of workers i.e. Frequency
$0 \leqslant t < 10$	21
$10 \leqslant t < 20$	14
$20 \leqslant t < 30$	28
$30 \leqslant t < 40$	8
$40 \leqslant t < 50$	4

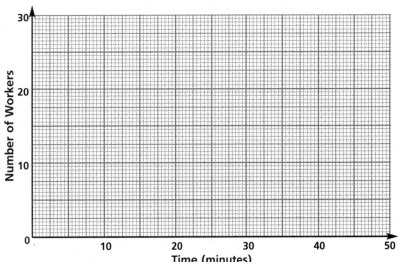

2 In a survey 50 women were asked how much they spend on cosmetics in one week.

The results are shown in the table below.

Money Spent, M (£)	Frequency
$0 \leqslant M < 2$	1
$2 \leqslant M < 4$	6
$4 \leqslant M < 6$	28
$6 \leqslant M < 8$	11
$8 \leqslant M < 10$	4

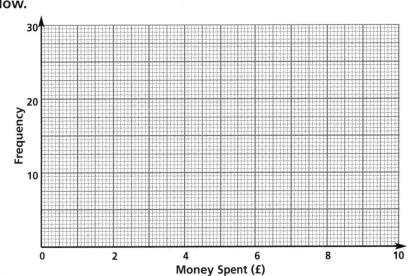

a) Draw a frequency polygon to show the information.

b) 50 men were also asked how much they spend on cosmetics in one week. The results are shown below. On the same axes draw a frequency polygon to show the amount of money spent by men.

Money Spent, M (£)	Frequency
$0 \leqslant M < 2$	13
$2 \leqslant M < 4$	28
$4 \leqslant M < 6$	5
$6 \leqslant M < 8$	3
$8 \leqslant M < 10$	1

c) How do the two distributions compare?

....

....

....

....

....

....

....

....

....

....

....

Displaying Data

1 The table below shows the distance that the workers at Barney's Biscuits have to travel to work.

a) Complete the frequency density column in the table.

b) Draw a histogram to illustrate the data in the table.

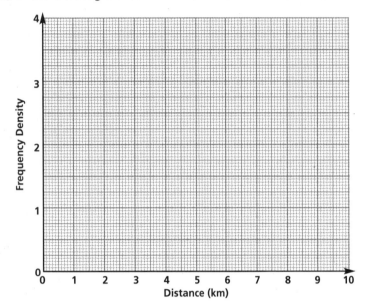

Distance (km)	Freq.	Freq. Density
$0 \leqslant d < 2$	7	3.5
$2 \leqslant d < 3$	3	
$3 \leqslant d < 4$	4	
$4 \leqslant d < 6$	3	
$6 \leqslant d < 10$	10	

2 The histogram opposite shows the distribution of the number of hours that students in Kim's class spent on a coursework task. How many students are there in Kim's class?

....

....

....

....

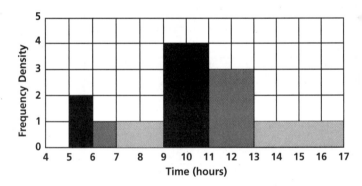

3 The dual bar chart shows sales of music downloads from an online music store.

a) Give a reason why sales were greatest in December. ....

b) The sales manager thinks that more men than women buy music downloads. Does the data support this? Show working to justify your answers.

....

....

....

....

....

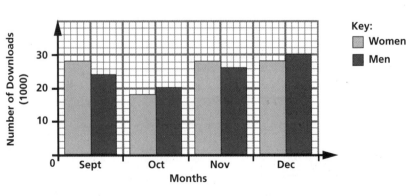

Displaying Data

1 This scatter diagram shows the average journey time and distance travelled for ten pupils travelling from home to school.

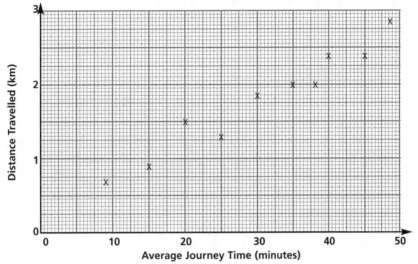

a) What does the scatter diagram tell you about the relationship between the journey time and the distance travelled?

....

b) Draw a line of best fit.

c) Use your graph to estimate…

    i) the time taken by John, who travelled a distance of 2.5 km. ....

    ii) the distance travelled by Donna, who takes 27 minutes. ....

2 The tables below show the heights and weights of 10 boys.

Height (cm)	133	162	130	163	153
Weight (kg)	70	84	64	87	87

Height (cm)	150	124	141	150	138
Weight (kg)	77	66	79	82	69

a) Use the information given to plot a scatter diagram, including line of best fit.

b) What type of correlation is there between height and weight?

....

c) i) Tony weighs 72kg. Use your graph to estimate his height. ....

    ii) Rob is 1.57m tall. Use your graph to estimate his weight. ....

Displaying Data

1 Below are the highest recorded temperatures, in °C, on one particular day for forty places around the world.

17, 28, 33, 19, 21, 28, 31, 24, 21, 20, 19, 28, 24, 19, 20, 24, 29, 32, 16, 26,

33, 24, 23, 16, 16, 20, 28, 17, 24, 23, 26, 31, 33, 18, 31, 26, 28, 19, 19, 21

a) Group together the data in a frequency table.

b) Construct a frequency diagram to show the data.

c) On separate axes construct a frequency polygon to show the data.

2 The students from Whitehall School took part in a fun run for charity. The table shows the times the students took to complete the run.

Time (min)	$40 \leqslant t < 60$	$60 \leqslant t < 70$	$70 \leqslant t < 80$	$80 \leqslant t < 90$	$90 \leqslant t < 100$	$100 \leqslant t < 120$
Frequency	28	43	58	40	34	18

a) Work out the frequency density.

b) Draw a histogram to illustrate this data.

3 The table gives information about the number of chapters and the total number of pages in books on Diane's shelf.

Number of chapters	19	28	11	14	27	23	8	16	21	25	32	19	35	11	16
Total number of pages	250	355	110	230	235	350	145	200	235	315	325	120	395	125	305

a) Use the information given to plot a scatter diagram, including a line of best fit.

b) What does the scatter diagram tell you about the relationship between the number of chapters and total number of pages?

c) Use your graph to estimate

i) the total number of pages if a book has 24 chapters

ii) the number of chapters if a book has a total of 190 pages

4 This table shows the number of telephone calls Mrs Chattergee makes in one week.

Day of the week	Monday	Tuesday	Wednesday	Thursday	Friday	Saturday	Sunday
Number of phone calls	3	2	8	4	7	10	6

a) Draw and label a pie chart to represent the information.

b) What percentage of the telephone calls were made at the weekend?

5 The table below shows the number of goals scored by the Year 11 football team in one season.

Number of goals scored	0	1	2	3	4	5	6
Number of games	7	5	11	3	3	0	1

a) What is **i)** the mean **ii)** the range **iii)** the mode **iv)** the median of the number of goals scored?

b) The Year 10 football team's mean was 2.2 goals per game in five fewer games. Which year scored the most goals and by how many?

6 During a PE lesson the boys have a 100m race. Their times were recorded and the results are shown below.

Time taken, t (seconds)	$12 < t \leqslant 14$	$14 < t \leqslant 16$	$16 < t \leqslant 18$	$18 < t \leqslant 20$	$20 < t \leqslant 22$	$22 < t \leqslant 24$
Number of boys	2	9	13	5	3	1

a) Calculate an estimate of the mean time

b) In which class interval does the median lie?

c) Which class interval is the mode?

Cumulative Frequency Diagrams

1 This cumulative frequency graph shows the time taken for 30 students to complete their maths homework.

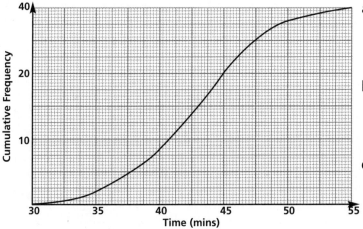

a) How many students took less than 40 minutes?

....

b) How many students took more than 40 minutes?

....

c) What was the median time taken?

....

2 Thirty five people took part in a skateboarding competition.

The points (*p*) they scored are shown in the table below.

Points scored (P)	Frequency	Cumulative Frequency
$0 < P \leqslant 5$	2	
$5 < P \leqslant 10$	4	
$10 < P \leqslant 15$	5	
$15 < P \leqslant 20$	7	
$20 < P \leqslant 25$	12	
$25 < P \leqslant 30$	5	

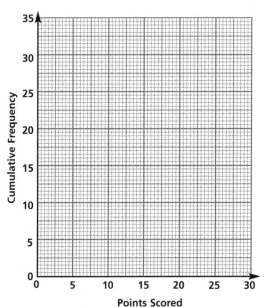

a) Complete the cumulative frequency column in the table.

b) Draw the cumulative frequency graph.

c) Use the graph to estimate…

    i) The median points scored ....

    ii) The interquartile range ....

d) How many competitors scored between 15 and 25 points?...

e) How many competitors scored more than 25 points? ....

f) Draw a box plot to illustrate this data.

Cumulative Frequency Diagrams

3 The heights in cm of 300 pupils were recorded as shown.

Height(h)	Frequency
$130 < h \leqslant 140$	10
$140 < h \leqslant 150$	39
$150 < h \leqslant 160$	95
$160 < h \leqslant 170$	125
$170 < h \leqslant 180$	31

a) Complete the table, adding a cumulative frequency column.

b) Draw the cumulative frequency curve.

c) Use your graph to find
   i) Median height
   ii) Interquartile range
   iii) Number of students taller than 155cm.

4 In one week a doctor weighed 80 men.
The table shows the results:

Weight	$50 < W \leqslant 60$	$60 < W \leqslant 70$	$70 < W \leqslant 80$	$80 < W \leqslant 90$	$90 < W \leqslant 100$
Frequency	11	27	29	8	5

a) Draw a cumulative frequency curve.

b) Use your graph to estimate...
   i) Median weight
   ii) Interquartile range

c) What percentage of men weighed more than 70kg?